Basic SPSS® Tutorial

⑤SAGE | 50 YEARS

SAGE was founded in 1965 by Sara Miller McCune to support the dissemination of usable knowledge by publishing innovative and high-quality research and teaching content. Today, we publish more than 750 journals, including those of more than 300 learned societies, more than 800 new books per year, and a growing range of library products including archives, data, case studies, reports, conference highlights, and video. SAGE remains majority-owned by our founder, and after Sara's lifetime will become owned by a charitable trust that secures our continued independence.

Los Angeles | London | Washington DC | New Delhi | Singapore | Boston

Basic SPSS® Tutorial

Manfred te Grotenhuis

Radboud University Nijmegen, the Netherlands

Anneke Matthijssen

Radboud University Nijmegen, the Netherlands

Los Angeles | London | New Delhi
Singapore | Washington DC | Boston

Los Angeles | London | New Delhi
Singapore | Washington DC | Boston

FOR INFORMATION:

SAGE Publications, Inc.
2455 Teller Road
Thousand Oaks, California 91320
E-mail: order@sagepub.com

SAGE Publications Ltd.
1 Oliver's Yard
55 City Road
London EC1Y 1SP
United Kingdom

SAGE Publications India Pvt. Ltd.
B 1/I 1 Mohan Cooperative Industrial Area
Mathura Road, New Delhi 110 044
India

SAGE Publications Asia-Pacific Pte. Ltd.
3 Church Street
#10-04 Samsung Hub
Singapore 049483

Printed in the United States of America

Cataloging-in-publication data is available for this title from the Library of Congress.

ISBN 978-1-4833-6941-9

This book is printed on acid-free paper.

SUSTAINABLE FORESTRY INITIATIVE
Certified Chain of Custody
Promoting Sustainable Forestry
www.sfiprogram.org
SFI-01268
SFI label applies to text stock

Acquisitions Editor: Vicki Knight
Editorial Assistant: Yvonne McDuffee
Associate Digital Content Editor: Katie Bierach
Production Editor: Kelly DeRosa
Copy Editor: QuADS Prepress (P) Ltd.
Typesetter: C&M Digitals (P) Ltd.
Proofreader: Wendy Jo Dymond
Cover Designer: Scott Van Atta
Marketing Manager: Nicole Elliott

15 16 17 18 19 10 9 8 7 6 5 4 3 2 1

Brief Contents

Detailed Contents

Preface

One of the most popular statistical programs of all times, **IBM**®
SPSS® **Statistics*** (which originally stood for **S**tatistical **P**ackage
for the **S**ocial **S**ciences), is a result of the project started in 1968 at
Stanford University, California. As a result of its immense popularity, it is
not surprising to find many SPSS textbooks being published. Most of these
books are voluminous because they combine SPSS with statistics. The need
to teach introductory courses in statistics, with a basic knowledge of SPSS,
at Radboud University Nijmegen, the Netherlands, however, called for an
abridged version of a textbook.

To achieve this purpose, we refrained from explaining statistical theory
almost completely and focused on the commands within the main menus of
SPSS instead. The Dutch manuscript was first introduced in 2002 and
adapted based on the teaching experiences as we progressed. The end
result was this textbook, which helps students understand SPSS, and more
important, to work with it. After reading and working with SPSS's commands, students are able to modify and analyze data with the most common
SPSS tools available.

Though all figures and instructions in this book are based on SPSS versions 20 to 22, the users of SPSS version 18 or 19 may not find much diffi-
culty in using it either.

This book is targeted to the audience who are novice users in SPSS. We
use clear-cut examples from real scientific research, while the reader is
invited to replicate the findings as he proceeds. The relevant outcomes
included may be used as a reference. Extra assignments are provided at the
end of each chapter that can be worked out by the students themselves,
without much external guidance, to enhance the effect of learning.

Manfred te Grotenhuis & Anneke Matthijssen
Radboud University Nijmegen, the Netherlands

---

*SPSS is a registered trademark of International Business Machines Corporation.

Acknowledgments

In 2002, I was requested by the faculty of social sciences of Radboud University Nijmegen in the Netherlands to reframe some statistical courses. The emphasis was shifted from theoretical knowledge toward practical applications, and this book is a result of that process. My thanks to Professor Scheepers, with whom I had discussions regarding simple methods to teach SPSS to social science students who wanted to apply statistics in their research but found it difficult. The Dutch version of this handbook was published mainly to cater to the needs of such students. Our intention was to remove fear from the minds of students who wanted to learn statistics and instill confidence in them. In the Netherlands, over the years, the Dutch version has become a best seller. It is part of the syllabi in five universities and in many college schools. The best compliment, however, came from a student of anthropology: "It is unbelievable that a subject as dull as statistics has been made so interesting!" Even after a decade this statement brings a smile on my face. I am also grateful to the University of Applied Sciences, Hengelo, the Netherlands for requesting me for an English edition in 2013, which paved the way for this international edition. Finally, I would like to thank Anita, Lotte, and Tommy for their love and concern.

—*Manfred te Grotenhuis*

As a student, even during my college days I got frustrated looking at the massive volumes of SPSS, which were not user friendly. The students who are not familiar with statistics found application of SPSS often difficult. It was during my internship and thesis that I got the opportunity to work on a more practical method to make learning SPSS easy. My thanks to Professor Scheepers for his valuable inputs and suggestions (in the Dutch version) regarding easy application of SPSS for students, which have been included in this book.

—*Anneke Matthijssen*

We express our gratitude to Matthew "Iron Man" Bennett for correcting our initial manuscripts and for providing indispensable inputs regarding the usage of English. We extend our special thanks to all the students from Radboud University Nijmegen, the Netherlands, whom we had the privilege to teach and who in turn contributed to the improvement of our lecture materials over the past 12 years. We thank the authorities in IBM SPSS who allowed us to use the screenshots of their program. Last but not least, we are most grateful to copyeditor Krishna Pradeep Joghee and the staff at SAGE Publications, in particular Vicki Knight, who immediately saw merits in this project.

The authors and SAGE Publications also acknowledge Robert Carter, University of Louisville; Patrick Kelly, Saint Louis University; Angela Pirlott, University of Wisconsin-Eau Claire; and Ayana Conway, Virginia State University, for their useful contributions to this text.

About the Authors

Manfred te Grotenhuis is an assistant professor of quantitative data analysis and an affiliate of the Interuniversity Center for Social Science Theory and Methodology (ICS). His has published statistical articles in prestigious journals such as *American Journal of Sociology*, *American Sociological Review*, *Demography*, the *Journal for the Scientific Study of Religion*, and the *International Journal of Epidemiology*. He has been teaching statistics at the faculty of Social Sciences at Radboud University, Nijmegen, the Netherlands since 1995 and has written several introductory books on SPSS and statistics. He is a recipient of the biennial University Teaching Award of Radboud University. He loves/hates to cycle a 20-mile time trial. He earned his PhD in sociology from Radboud University Nijmegen, the Netherlands.

Anneke Matthijssen started her career as a medical analyst. She was involved in teaching statistics even during her study and after graduating at the Radboud University as well. Since 2008, she works as a policy advisor/institutional researcher at the strategy and development department of the Radboud University. In her position as policy advisor, she provides the board and faculties with management information on education and research. She is also the secretary of the Dutch association for institutional researchers, which comprises the policy advisors of all Dutch universities. Unlike Manfred, she loves cycling in the mountains of Italy. She completed her MSc in educational sciences from Radboud University Nijmegen, the Netherlands.

Chapter 1
Statistics Program SPSS

1.1 What Is SPSS? △

SPSS (Statistical Package for the Social Sciences) is a popular program to describe and analyze statistical data. The drop-down menus in SPSS makes it easier for users to carry out all statistical procedures. This tutorial will help you learn the basic features to load, modify, and analyze data. Using examples from a school evaluation survey, we illustrate a number of common SPSS functions. Each example contains a detailed description of the menu-driven computer commands, and readers are invited to carry these out themselves to learn by *doing*. The results of all these commands are displayed in figures and tables. This enables students to work with SPSS program practically on their own, without any prior knowledge of the program.

This book focuses mainly on the SPSS program itself and not much on the statistical theory underlying the many procedures. For a comprehensive introduction to statistics, we would like you to refer to the textbook *Discovering Statistics With SPSS* by Andy Field.

1.2 The Purpose of SPSS △

Statistics can be divided into two categories: (1) descriptive statistics and (2) inferential statistics. Descriptive statistics simply describes the data from a certain population, while inferential statistics is concerned with making predictions or statements about a population, based on data from a sample, which is a part of that population.

As a program, SPSS is similar to a fast and sophisticated calculator with great capabilities, allowing us to run statistical procedures in the field of descriptive and inferential statistics. A number of these procedures are covered in this book.

In conducting scientific research, the application of statistical analysis software like SPSS is essential. In the research process, SPSS is used when the data need to be entered, processed, and analyzed. The key objective of this book is to enable users to

1. enter and process research data with SPSS and
2. to carry out a number of common procedures within SPSS.

△ 1.3 Structure of the Book

In this chapter, we first describe the program and the way it is structured. In Chapters 2 to 5, we describe how to load data into SPSS, modify the data, and apply commonly used descriptive and inferential statistics. Each of the chapters is divided into sections, which address a particular topic in the field. In each section, we first describe an SPSS function, provide an example, and then show how to use the SPSS point-and-click commands in the drop-down menus. The description of all commands in this book is preceded by the ⌨ symbol and placed in a "box" to separate them from the normal text, so that they can be easily located. For easy reference, all relevant results ("output") are displayed immediately after the instructions and commands. To enhance the effects of learning by doing, each chapter also contains extra assignments where the reader is invited to modify and analyze data without much external guidance.

△ 1.4 Fictitious Data Set

Working with real-life examples makes the task of mastering the common SPSS applications easier. That is why for practice we use a data set, which is freely available on the web (study.sagepub.com/basicspss). The data set contains fictitious, yet realistic, data from students who have filled out a questionnaire (evaluation form) after having taken a statistics course. The following information is available in the data set:

Background characteristics

AGE	students' age measured in years
SEX	code: male = 0, female = 1
STUDY	pedagogical sciences = 0, educational sciences = 1
ENROLL	full-time = 0, part-time = 1

Computer skills

COMPU1	word processing (1 = very poor, . . . , 5 = very good)
COMPU2	handling spreadsheets (1 = very poor, . . . , 5 = very good)
COMPU3	using Windows (1 = very poor, . . . , 5 = very good)

School-related activities

HOMEWORK	time spent on doing home work in hours
PRACTICE	number of SPSS practice lessons attained
THEORY	number of statistical theory lessons attained

Exams

| GRADE | final grade received for a course in statistics |

In this book, we assume that the data are stored in a folder named **SPSS Basics**. Of course, the reader is free to choose another folder if he or she wishes to do so.

1.5 Using the Windows in SPSS △

SPSS uses a variety of bars and drop-down menus. Before we actually learn to start the program in Chapter 2, we first give a brief description of the main structure and the basic menu options.

1.5.1 The Bars and Drop-Down Menus

After SPSS gets started, a data window will appear (see Figure 1.1). This window contains four bars: (1) title bar, (2) menu bar, (3) toolbar, and (4) status bar.

1. The **title bar** contains the name of the file that has been opened.
2. The **menu bar** contains the main SPSS menus.
3. The **toolbar** allows you to select the SPSS tasks.
4. The **status bar** lets you know in what stage the program is in.

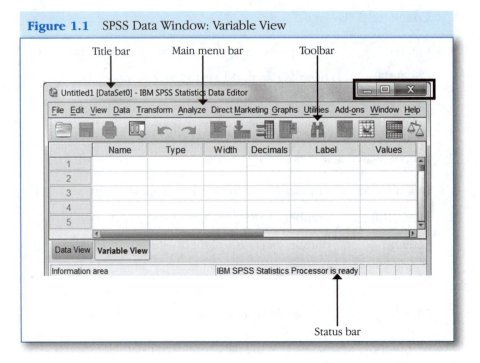

Figure 1.1 SPSS Data Window: Variable View

1.5.2 Title Bar

The title bar is located at the top of the data window and contains three buttons on the right-hand side (see box in Figure 1.1). The far right (red) button is the system button. One click on this button does close down SPSS. The button in the center is the resize button, enlarging or shrinking the window. With one click, the left-hand button minimizes the data window to an icon on the Windows toolbar. Clicking on the icon again will bring back the SPSS data window to its original size.

1.5.3 Main Menu Bar

The main menu bar is located directly below the title bar and is the core of the program. Clicking on the bar's titles will open a specific drop-down menu, with the menu options becoming visible. Options in black may be selected whereas options marked in gray cannot be selected at that time. Each menu contains options on a number of related SPSS components. For example, the **File** menu contains all options dealing with files like opening, saving, and printing. The arrow (▶) that follows an option indicates that a second option must be selected. An option followed by three periods, for example, **Select Cases** . . . in the **Data** menu, means that a dialog window will open after choosing that option. The main menu bar holds the following drop-down menus:

- *File* This menu contains all options related to opening, creating, saving, and printing SPSS files. It also includes options to import files from other software packages.
- *Edit* This contains options to edit or copy the content of various windows and to change the default setup of SPSS.
- *View* Here users may change the screen setup. A popular option is **Value labels** to switch on and off category labels.
- *Data* This menu contains options to describe and modify variables, as well as to select and sort data.
- *Transform* Here users can create new variables, often on the basis of existing variables.
- *Analyze* This key menu contains statistical procedures of SPSS and is subdivided into submenus containing all sorts of statistical operations.
- *Direct marketing* This is an advanced menu used for market analysis.
- *Graphs* This menu contains options for creating various charts and graphs such as histograms, bar charts, and scatterplots.
- *Utilities* This contains the **variables** option, among other things, which allows users to quickly retrieve details from their data.
- *Add ons* This menu contains links to additional options outside the standard package.
- *Window* This allows users to determine which window is active—that is, which window is opened and can be used.
- *Help* An extensive help menu that operates similar to other help options in other Windows application.

1.5.4 Toolbar

The toolbar is located directly below the menu bar; it contains buttons that execute commands directly. On the left-hand side are the central command buttons, which are active in all SPSS windows. The right-hand side contains window-specific buttons. When the cursor is moved to a specific point, the button will highlight and provide a brief description of its function.

1.5.5 Status Bar

The status bar at the bottom of the screen provides details about operations being run by SPSS at that time. If the program is idle, the message "IBM SPSS Statistics Processor is ready" will appear in the status bar (see Figure 1.1). Messages may appear on the bar concerning operations that are being run, such as the following:

- *Filter on*   This means that only a selection (subset) of cases will be analyzed.
- *Split file on*   This means that operations will be run separately for specific groups in the file.

△   1.6   Using SPSS Windows

In SPSS, the two most important windows are related to the data and to the output of statistical procedures. Users can have multiple windows open at any time. However, as in other programs, users can only work in the window active at that time. Data and output windows can be activated by selecting the **Window** option in the menu bar.

1.6.1 Data Window

The data window, which is the window you will see first after starting the program, gives an overview of the data that have been loaded into the program. By default, the window is empty (see Figure 1.1). The user has two options: (1) to enter new data by typing them into the empty cells or (2) to load existing data files. All data, which were obtained through a survey, for instance, can be loaded or entered into this window that works as a data sheet. The information (i.e., scores on variables) from each respondent is displayed in rows (see the horizontal rectangle in Figure 1.2). The values of each variable, for example, "age," are displayed in columns (see the vertical rectangle in Figure 1.2). These data are the raw material used for descriptive or inferential statistical analyses.

Figure 1.2 Data Window: Data View

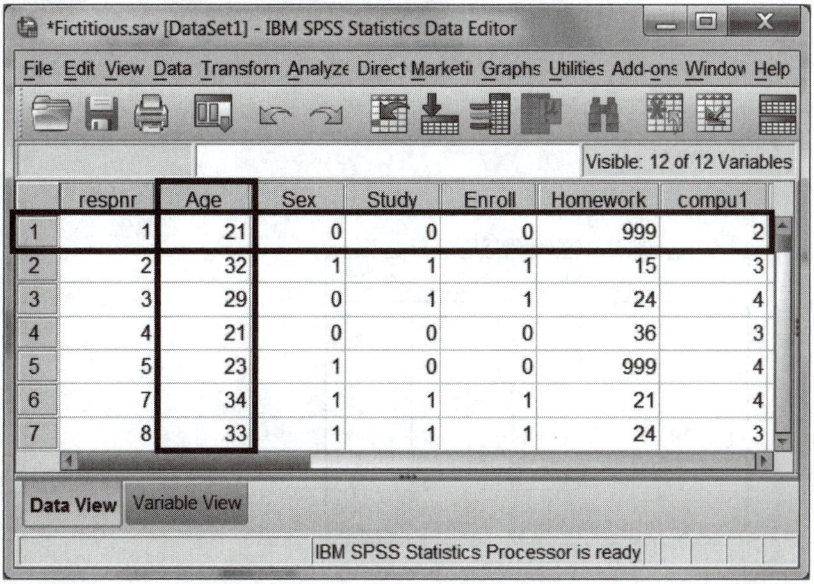

	respnr	Age	Sex	Study	Enroll	Homework	compu1
1	1	21	0	0	0	999	2
2	2	32	1	1	1	15	3
3	3	29	0	1	1	24	4
4	4	21	0	0	0	36	3
5	5	23	1	0	0	999	4
6	7	34	1	1	1	21	4
7	8	33	1	1	1	24	3

Note: Displays seven rows with data.

1.6.2 Output Window

This window shows the results of all the operations run with SPSS during a session (i.e., the time between opening and closing SPSS). Once SPSS gets started, the output window is not in use and will only open after a command has been given.

Example

After requesting a frequency distribution of the variable "age," the content of the output window will look like the one in Figure 1.3.

Note that SPSS displays the age of the students (between 18 and 30 years), the absolute numbers, and the relative shares. For example, there are three 20-year-old students, who constitute 8.1% of all students in the data set.

Figure 1.3 Output Window

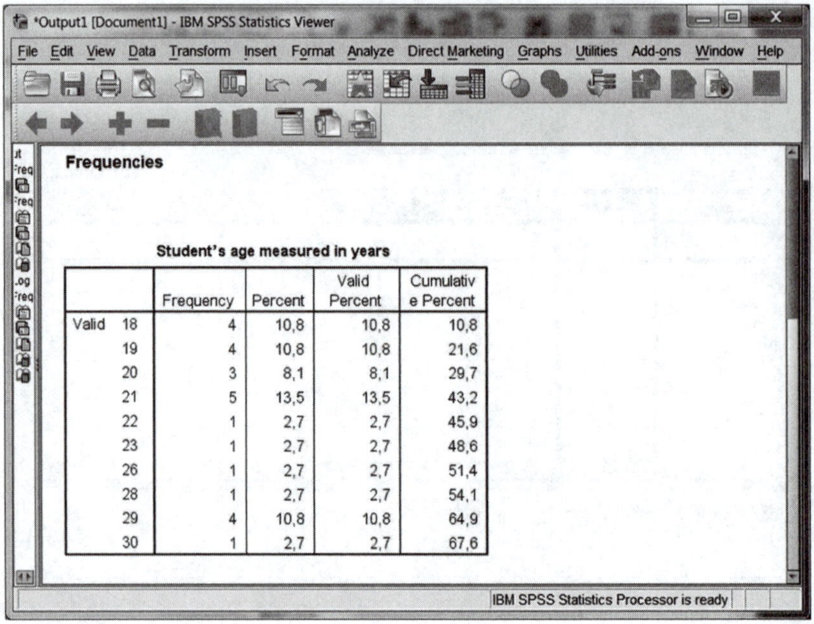

Student's age measured in years

		Frequency	Percent	Valid Percent	Cumulative Percent
Valid	18	4	10,8	10,8	10,8
	19	4	10,8	10,8	21,6
	20	3	8,1	8,1	29,7
	21	5	13,5	13,5	43,2
	22	1	2,7	2,7	45,9
	23	1	2,7	2,7	48,6
	26	1	2,7	2,7	51,4
	28	1	2,7	2,7	54,1
	29	4	10,8	10,8	64,9
	30	1	2,7	2,7	67,6

Note: Displays the frequency table for "age," 18 to 30 years.

△ 1.7 SPSS File Types

Every window in SPSS has its own file type, which can be recognized by its file extension. In this book, we use

- data files that are saved using the .sav extension (e.g., *Chapter1.sav*) and
- output files with results from the output window that are saved with a .spv extension (e.g., *Chapter1.spv*).

In the next chapter, we take a closer look at opening, editing, saving, and retrieving such files.

Chapter 2

SPSS Files

2.1 Introduction △

Data files play a key role in SPSS. Naturally, the data in these files can be obtained in various ways. To keep things simple, we use data obtained through the evaluations forms that were handed to students after a statistics course was taken. The data of this particular study can be stored in three different ways:

1. The data might have already been stored in an SPSS data file. The file needs to be opened only for modifications and/or for statistical analyses (see Section 2.2).
2. The data may not be digitized; the information may be available only on the filled-out (paper) forms. Thus, a data file must be created (see Section 2.3).
3. The results may be entered into a digital file using a spreadsheet program, like the popular program EXCEL. This file must be converted to an SPSS data file (see Section 2.4).

2.2 Open SPSS Files △

- Open SPSS using the SPSS icon on your desktop or via Start, Programs ▶; click on the IBM SPSS folder; and then on the SPSS program.
- If the SPSS welcome window appears, close it by clicking **Cancel**.
- After the empty SPSS data window appears, go to the menu bar and select: **File**
                 Open ▶ and click **Data** . . .

The dialog window "Open Data" will appear (see Figure 2.1).

Figure 2.1 Dialog Window "Open Data"

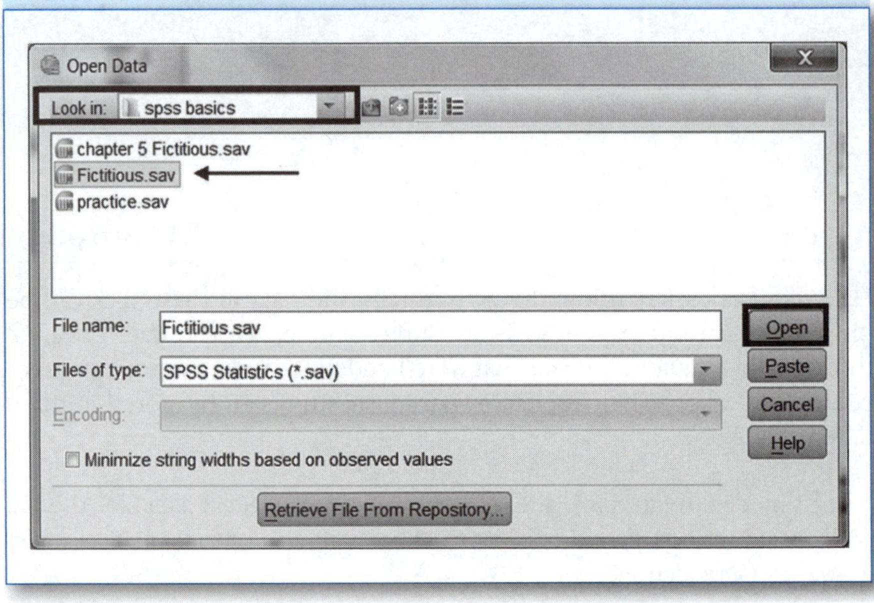

• Select the correct folder in "Look in:" (**SPSS Basics** in this case) and open the file *Fictitious.sav* directly with a double-click on the name or by selecting (one click) and clicking **Open** (see Figure 2.1).

If the output window appears instead of the data window, then

• Click **Window** in the menu bar and click on *Fictitious.sav* to activate the file.

Similarly, the output files can be opened, and they contain the results from commands that have been previously executed. Open the following output file using the instructions in the following box:

- From the menu bar, select   **File**
                                   Open ▶ and click **Output** . . .

The accompanying dialog window will appear.

- If necessary, select the right drive and the **SPSS Basics** folder.
- Double-click to open the file *output.spv*.

This file shows the age distribution of 37 students in total. They are aged between 18 and 37 years. Four students are 18 years old, which is 10.8% of the total (37). Two students are 37 years old, which is 5.4% of the total.

2.3 Create and Modify Data Files △

Research material supplied as filled-out registration forms on paper must first be converted to digital data sheets. However, before any data can be entered into such a data sheet, variables must be created. This is called *data definition*. This means that the questions from the survey or questionnaire are to be converted to variables, which have to be named, and eventually, more information about the variable must be added (labeling). After all questions have been converted to variables with a name (and a label), you may begin to enter the scores (values) related to those variables into the spreadsheet. In the following sections, we show how this is done.

2.3.1 Define and Create Variables

After starting the program, SPSS opens an empty data window by default. However, in the current situation, the file *fictitious.sav* is open and active (see Section 2.2). To open an empty data window now, follow the instructions below:

Select from the menu bar   **File**
                               New ▶ **Data**

The data view window (Figure 1.2) or the variable window (Figure 2.2) opens, depending on the way SPSS was used in the previous session. If the data view window is open, follow the instruction below first:

From the bottom bar, select **Variable View**.

The data window now has changed to *variable view*, where the information is listed on all variables; see Figure 2.2.

Figure 2.2 An Empty Data Window

Toggle between the data window (Data View) and the variable window (Variable View)

Note: The Variable View window is active.

Before entering the data, it is a standard procedure to first indicate (define) which variables are used. We explain this in the following example.

Example

Suppose you want to define two variables related to the survey questions (1) "How much time do you spend per month doing statistics homework?" and (2) "Is the student male or female?" The names for these two variables are chosen to be (1) "homework" and (2) "sex."

- Double-click on the empty cell beneath **Name** (see Figure 2.2).
- Subsequently, enter the name of the variable (*homework*) and press [**Enter**] on the keyboard.
- Double-click on the empty cell beneath *homework* and fill in *sex* and again press [**Enter**].

The results are shown in Figure 2.3. Note that we use only words for the variable names. The variable names in SPSS always begin with a letter (a number as first character is not allowed) and may be succeeded by a maximum of 63 letters or numbers. Furthermore, SPSS does not allow for spaces/blanks or symbols (except an underscore [_]) in a variable name. So "home work," "home+work," and "1homework" cannot be used. Once used, you cannot repeat the same name for yet another variable, so each name must be unique.

Figure 2.3 Data Window With Variables "homework" and "sex" Defined

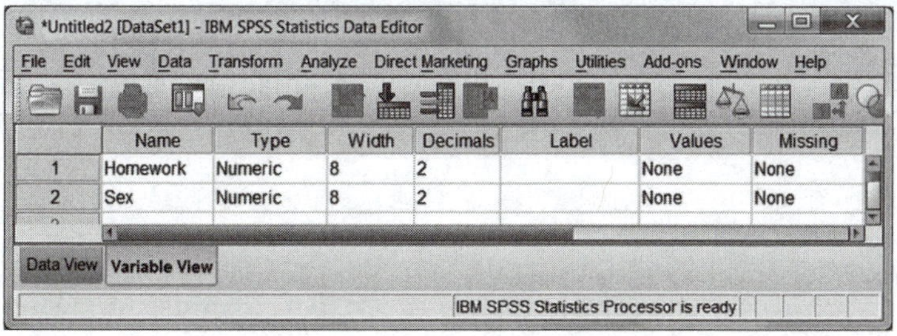

Similarly, other features of variables can be changed (if needed):

- **Type**   This is the variable type: numeric (numbers) or—less frequent—string (text); the default type is numeric.
- **Width**   The maximum number of characters that can be shown in the Data View window; 8 is the default width.
- **Decimals**   The maximum number of decimals that can be shown in the Data View window; 2 is the default number of decimals.

As illustrated in Figure 2.3, SPSS enters the default settings for type = numeric, width = 8, and decimals = 2. These settings may be left unchanged here.

2.3.2 Add Variable Labels

It is common practice to provide a more detailed description of the variables if the variable name itself is not enough. This can be done by using the **Label** option in the Variable View window (see the example below).

Example

The variable that denotes the average time spent by a student on statistics homework (in minutes) has been defined as "homework" in the column **Name** in the data window. The **Label** column indicates the time spent at home in hours (Figure 2.4).

To add labels to variables, follow these instructions:

- Select the first empty cell beneath **Label** with a double-click.

You may enter a more detailed description of the variable in up to 255 characters here: *time spent on homework statistics in hours.*

- Enter our detailed definition and then press [**Enter**].

Figure 2.4   Add Labels to Variables

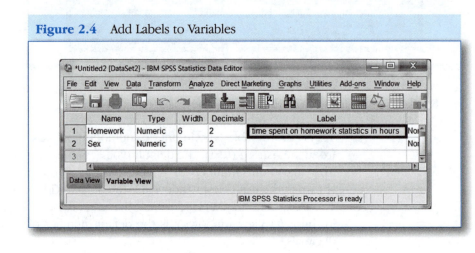

2.3.3 Add Value Labels

Besides variable labels, the codes or categories of the variable are also often labeled to avoid confusion.

Example

In the data view window, there is a variable named "sex." This variable, of course, has two categories: (1) male = 0 and (2) female = 1. Labeling the categories as 0 and 1 is useful, given that the information will be displayed in any relevant SPSS output. For example, when viewing a frequency distribution of the variable "sex," displaying 0 and 1 is not enough. So we have to add the appropriate names to the codes to remove the uncertainty of the meaning of 0 and 1.

- Select **None** in the second cell beneath **Values** (this is a cell from the row marked as "sex").
- Click on the icon ⬛ to the right of **None**.

The dialog window "Value Labels" will now appear (see Figure 2.5).

Figure 2.5 Dialog Window "Value Labels"

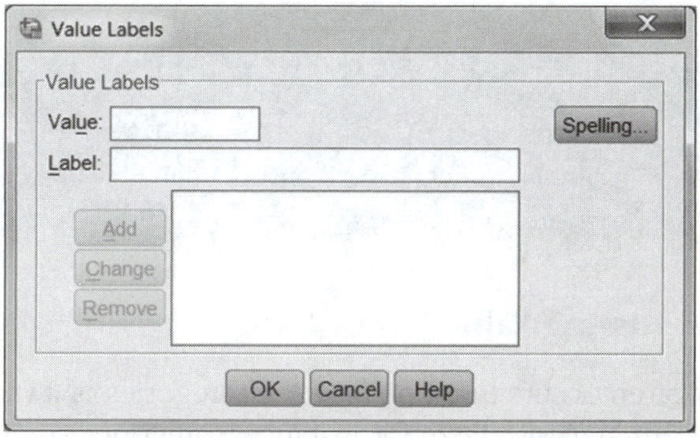

- Enter the number 0 into the empty box right of **Value**. Then, select the box that follows **Label** and enter *male*.
- Click **Add** to label 0 = male.
- Now, enter 1 in the **Value** box and *female* in the **Label** box.
- And again click on **Add** to add 1 = female.

Check whether you have followed the instructions correctly with Figure 2.6 as a reference.

Figure 2.6 Dialog Window "Value Labels" With Labels Added

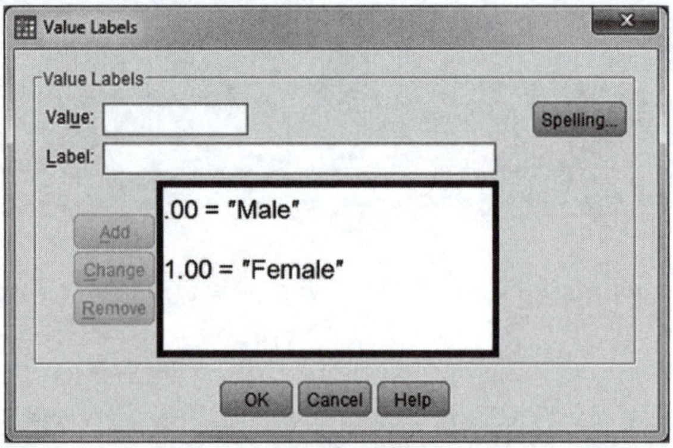

Click on **OK** to finish ("sex" now has the correct value labels).

2.3.4 Define Missing Values

In research, it often occurs that one or more categories of a variable need to be excluded from analysis. Take, for instance, categories such as "not filled in," "I don't know," or extremely low or high scores (so-called outliers). You can exclude such categories in SPSS by listing these categories as missing (invalid) values. These values are then not included in any analysis. To list the invalid scores, the dialog window "Missing Values" is used (see Figure 2.7).

Example

In case of the variable "homework," where respondents were asked to list the time they spent on statistics homework, a number of them did not answer, maybe because they did not keep track of how much time they spent doing homework or they simply could not remember. For this group of students, we use the value 999, a value that falls way out of the range of possible answers to that question, so it can be easily detected.

- Select **None** in the first cell beneath **Missing** in the Variable View window (this row is named as "homework").
- Then, click ▦ to the right of **None**.

The "Missing Values" dialog window will appear; see Figure 2.7.

Figure 2.7 Dialog Window "Missing Values"

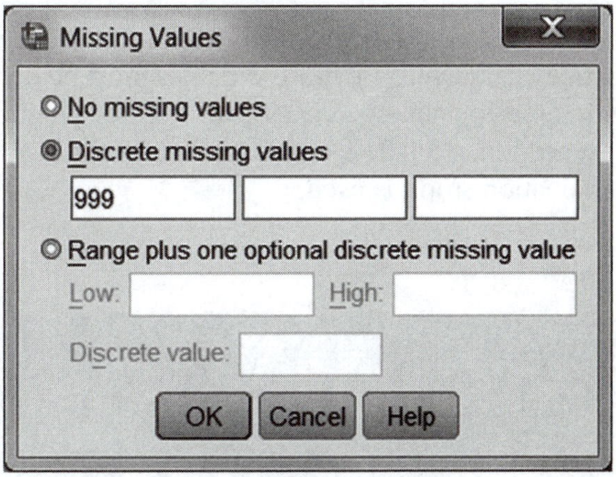

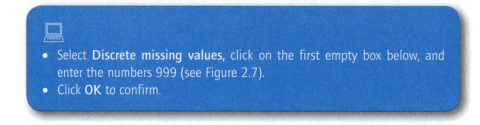

- Select **Discrete missing values,** click on the first empty box below, and enter the numbers 999 (see Figure 2.7).
- Click **OK** to confirm.

If you followed all instructions correctly, the variable view window will look like the one (see the last column [Missing]) in Figure 2.8.

Figure 2.8   Data Window: Variable View (active)

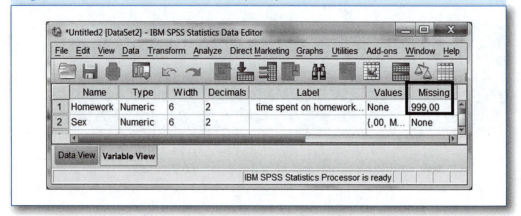

Note: The variables "homework" and "sex" with 999 is defined as "missing" in "homework."

The information regarding the two variables has now been entered into the file. In practice, of course, a lot more variables must be defined this way. As this is a fairly time-consuming process, we will not pursue this any further. In the next section, a full-fledged file, including all variables of the statistics course evaluation study, is used.

2.3.5 Enter Data

- Open the data file *practice.sav*. See Section 2.2 for the relevant instructions.
- If the Variable View window opens (Figure 2.8), click on **Data View** in the bottom left-hand corner of the variable window.

After this, the SPSS data view window is active (see Figure 2.9). This window is a type of spreadsheet, made up of rows and columns. The respondents (students in this case) are placed in the various rows, with the variables being listed in columns. The places where rows and columns intersect are called *cells*. Each of these cells contains one single score. The cell that is selected with the computer mouse is called the *active cell*. You can activate a cell by pointing the computer mouse on it and then clicking it with the left mouse button.

The active cell is the only cell in which data can be entered or altered. The content of an active cell is always displayed in the *Cell Editor*, which is the white box at the top of the spreadsheet. When you enter data into a cell, it always shows up first in the Cell Editor. In order to actually enter the data into the active cell, you have to hit the [**Enter**] or [**Tab**] key or activate another cell with the cursor.

Figure 2.9 Data Window: Data View (active)

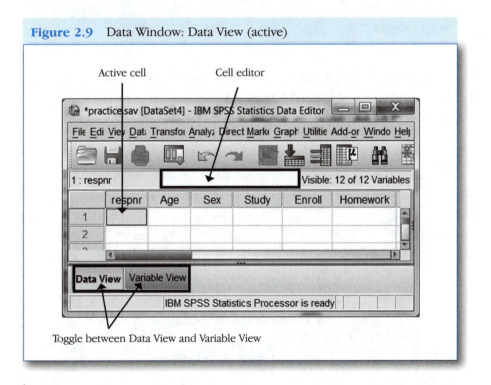

The conventional procedure is to enter all the scores (other words are values or codes) case by case. Here, the cases are students. The data for just one case (one student) are normally displayed in one single row of the data sheet.

> ⌨
>
> Select the first empty cell beneath the first variable ("respnr").

The cell will turn yellow and is activated (see Figure 2.9). You may now enter the score for this variable. In this case, it is the variable called "respnr" (respondent identification number), which serves to identify each student. The value or score for the first student then is 1.

> ⌨
>
> • Enter the value 1 into the empty cell below "respnr."
> • Hit [**Tab**] on the keyboard.

The value 1 that you have entered is displayed in the active cell, and the first cell beneath "age" is active now (see Figure 2.10).

Figure 2.10   Data Window: First Number Entered (respnr = 1)

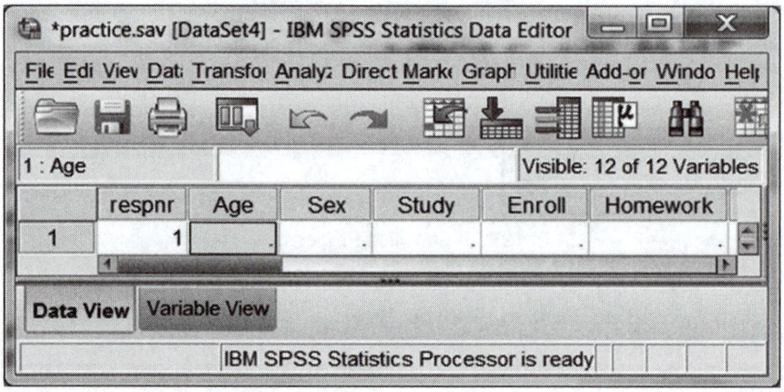

Note: respnr = respondent identification number.

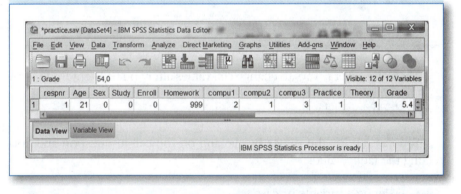

- Our first student is a 21-year-old male, studies pedagogical sciences, and is full-time enrolled. He did not answer how much time he spent on statistics homework, has poor skills working with word processing, has very poor skills working with spreadsheets, has average experience using Windows, attended one practice session and one theory lecture, and received a 5.4 as his final grade. Check pages 23-24 to see how the values/codes match the preceding information and enter them into the correct cells. *Note:* Computers with language settings (see Windows Control Panel) other than English may only accept 5,4 and not 5.4.

After you have entered the values, the data view window will look like the one in Figure 2.11:

Figure 2.11   Data View Window: Data of First Student Entered

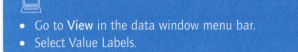

- Go to **View** in the data window menu bar.
- Select Value Labels.

Check whether the content of your own data window matches that of Figure 2.12 and verify whether the student (respondent 1) is indeed male, studies pedagogical sciences, is enrolled full-time, gave no answer about time spent on homework, has poor word processing skills, has very poor experience handling spreadsheets and has average experience working with Windows, attended one practice session, one theory lecture and received a 5.4 as his final grade. If any cells do not match, then change the related cell value (for an explanation, see the instructions below Figure 2.12) until everything is correct. You do not have to save the file; this was just an exercise to learn how to enter data.

Figure 2.12   Data Window: Data View Active and "value labels" Checked

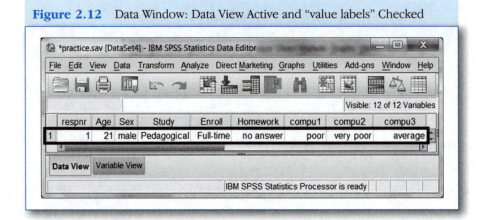

There are several ways to change cell values after you have entered them:

- Modifying cell values

You can modify the values by clicking on the cell in question and correcting the faulty value:

- Deleting a variable or case

You can delete a variable (column) or case (row) by clicking on the variable name at the top of the column or on the row number on the left-hand side and subsequently hitting [**Delete**] on your keyboard.

△ 2.4 Load Excel Files

It is common practice to enter and store data onto a computer with programs other than SPSS. The fictitious data set we are using in this book was originally just a collection of rows and columns with numbers (see the following example). There are many so-called spreadsheet programs that can store this type of data. One particularly popular spreadsheet program is EXCEL, which is part of the Microsoft Office package. Such files can easily be converted into SPSS data files.

Basically, EXCEL files are made up of a matrix of numbers in rows and columns. The data of one single respondent is displayed in each row. In our example, it contains the research material from the students who filled in the evaluation form. These data can be used to run statistical analyses not only within EXCEL itself but also in SPSS.

Example

The first five rows of research material (the answers of students 1 to 5) looks like the following:

1	21	0	0	0	999	2	1	3	1	1	5.4
2	32	1	1	1	15	3	1	1	3	4	3.9
3	29	0	1	1	24	4	3	3	2	3	2.8
4	21	0	0	0	36	3	2	3	2	3	7.3
5	23	1	0	0	999	4	4	3	5	5	5.0

The data above are the answers to questions in an evaluation form that have been entered into an EXCEL file. Each column (divided by spaces) provides the data for a single variable. Each row provides the answers for every student separately. In the 12 columns we have the values for the following (12) variables:

1. Student's identifier code (random unique number)
2. Student's age (measured in years)
3. Sex (0 = male, 1 = female)
4. Study (0 = pedagogical sciences, 1 = educational sciences)
5. Enrollment (0 = full-time, 1= part-time)
6. Time spent on homework (in minutes) (no answer = 999)
7. Word processing skills (Word) (1 = very poor, 2 = poor, 3 = average, 4 = good, 5 = very good)
8. Experience working with spreadsheets (Excel) (1 = very poor, 2 = poor, 3 = average, 4 = good, 5 = very good)
9. Experience working with Windows (1 = very poor, 2 = poor, 3 = average, 4 = good, 5 = very good)

10. Number of practice sessions attended
11. Number of lectures attended
12. Final grade received for the statistics course

Consequently, we can say that the student in the first row on page 23—remember it is the one you had already entered into the *practice.sav* file during an exercise in the previous section—is a 21-year-old male, studies pedagogical sciences, is enrolled full-time, gives no answer on time spent on statistics homework, has poor word processing skills, has very poor skills handling spreadsheets, has average experience working with Windows, attends one practice and one lecture, and received a 5.4 as his final grade for the statistics course.

As mentioned earlier, the data files that have been created with other software can be converted to SPSS data files. This is generally known as *importing* data and basically involves a process that is similar to opening an SPSS data file with a .sav extension.

SPSS can handle a great many data file types. The most widely used types are

- SPSS data files for other operating systems, for example, Macintosh and Unix (extension: *.por*);
- text files (extension: *.txt*); and
- EXCEL files (extension: *.xls of .xlsx*).

For a complete overview of file types, see Figure 2.13.

As Excel is widely used, we will now demonstrate how Excel files can be imported in SPSS.

- Go to **File**
  Open ▶ and click **Data** . . .
- If necessary, select the correct drive and folder (**SPSS Basics**) and to the right of **Files of type** click ▼ and select Excel as file type; see Figure 2.13 for reference.
- Now double-click on *Excelfile.xlsx* (see Figure 2.14). The dialog window "Opening Excel Data Source" will appear (see Figure 2.15).

Figure 2.13 Dialog Window "Open Data"

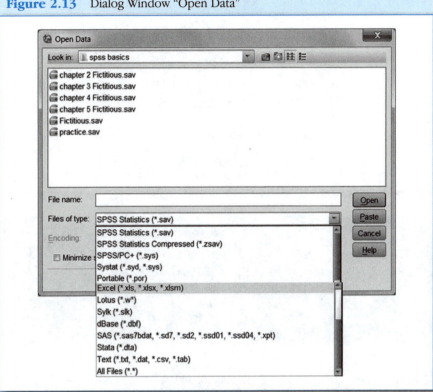

Figure 2.14 Dialog Window "Open Data," Files of Type: Excel

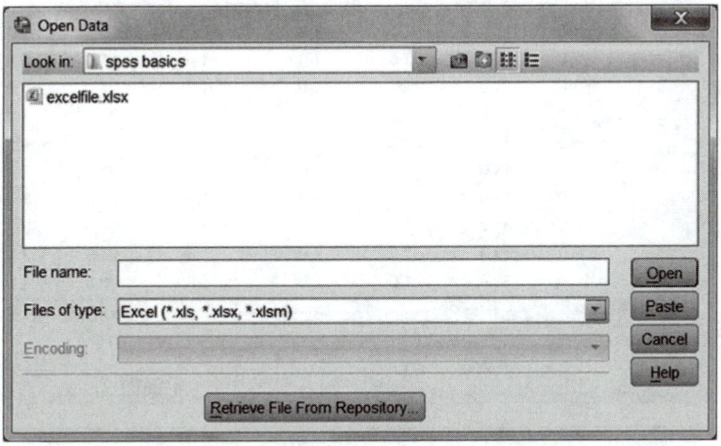

Figure 2.15 Dialog Window "Opening Excel Data Source"

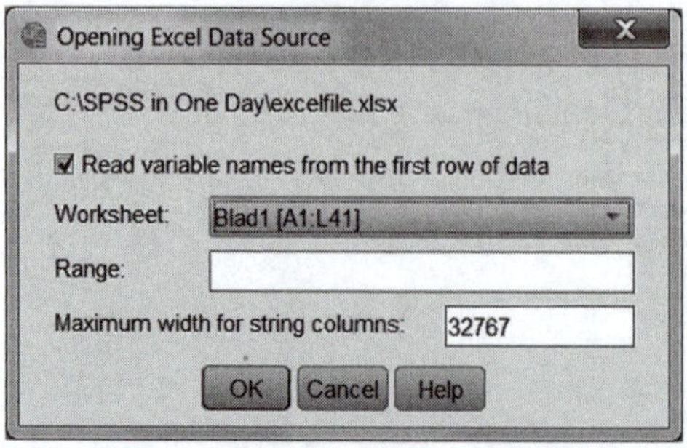

- Leave "read variable names from the first row of data" checked (the Excel file has already [short] names for the variables in the first row).
- Then, click **OK**. The data will be loaded into SPSS (see Figure 2.16 for reference).

Figure 2.16 Data Window: Excel File Loaded

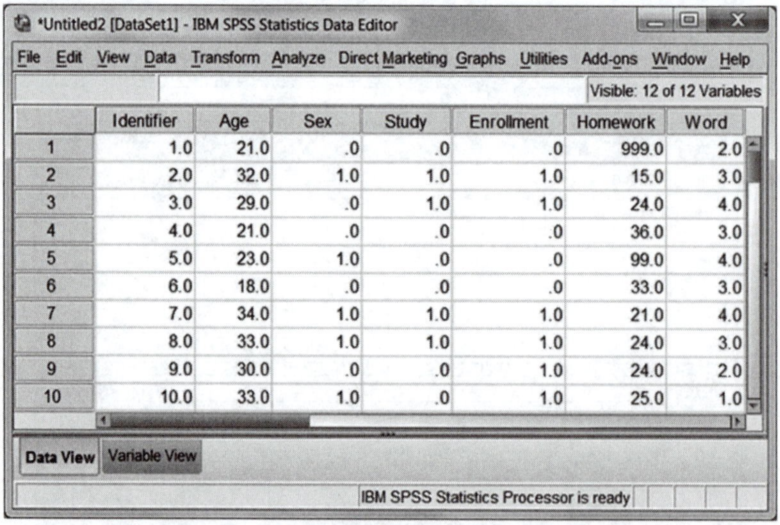

	Identifier	Age	Sex	Study	Enrollment	Homework	Word
1	1.0	21.0	.0	.0	.0	999.0	2.0
2	2.0	32.0	1.0	1.0	1.0	15.0	3.0
3	3.0	29.0	.0	1.0	1.0	24.0	4.0
4	4.0	21.0	.0	.0	.0	36.0	3.0
5	5.0	23.0	1.0	.0	.0	99.0	4.0
6	6.0	18.0	.0	.0	.0	33.0	3.0
7	7.0	34.0	1.0	1.0	1.0	21.0	4.0
8	8.0	33.0	1.0	1.0	1.0	24.0	3.0
9	9.0	30.0	.0	.0	1.0	24.0	2.0
10	10.0	33.0	1.0	.0	1.0	25.0	1.0

Note: Displays the first 10 rows.

2.5 Save SPSS Files △

If all data have been entered correctly and have been provided with labels, and so on, then, the entire file can be saved as an SPSS data file.

- Go to **Window** in the menu bar and check whether the imported Excel file (named "Untitled") is active. SPSS allows multiple data files to be open, although only one can be active at a time—this is indicated by the tick in front of the file name (this chapter has up to four data files open).
- Go to **File** in the menu bar and select **Save As** . . .

The dialog window "Save Data As" (Figure 2.17) opens:

Figure 2.17   Dialog Window "Save Data As"

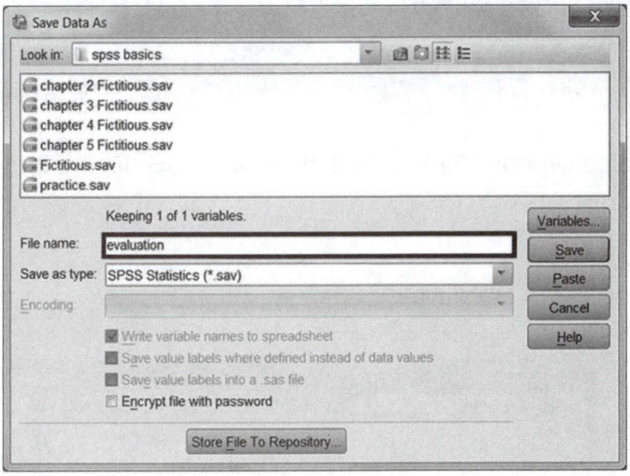

Now carry out the following instructions to save the file that was opened in Section 2.4 (name: *excelfile.xlsx*) as a .sav file:

- If needed, select the correct drive and folder, which in this case is **SPSS Basics**.
- Type the relevant file name into the box (*evaluation*).
- You do not have to type the extension .sav; this is added automatically by SPSS!
- Now execute the command by clicking **Save**. You have now saved the Excel data file *excelfile.xlsx* as a more accessible and informative SPSS .sav file.
- Please note that you can also save the data as an Excel file. You may click on ▼ to the right of **Save as type** to find the possible programs.

You can save your output in a similar way:

- Go to **Window** in the menu bar and select the output window called **Output1**.
- Then, from the menu bar, go to   **File**
                                          Save As . . .

The dialog window "Save as" will then open (see Figure 2.18).

Figure 2.18   Save SPSS Output

- In the **File name** box, type the relevant file name, which in this case is *firstoutput* (do not add an extension).
- Complete the task by clicking "**Save**."

In this chapter, you learned how to handle data in SPSS. Since you are new to the program, we guided you through all operations. We believe that you learn SPSS best by doing. The effect is strongest when after some practice you do it on your own with minimum guidance. This is why we end every chapter with some exercises that are related to the previous sections with less assistance and guidelines.

2.6 Assignments △

1. SPSS allows for multiple data windows to be open at any given time. The file that was opened in Section 2.2, that is, *fictitious.sav*, is still present but not active. You can activate it again by selecting **Window** in the menu bar and subsequently, clicking on *fictitious.sav*. If needed, switch to Variable View (see page 12 and Figure 2.2).

2. The data set is incomplete:

   - First of all, not all names of the variables in the file are correct. Rename V1 into *sex*, V2 into *homework*, and V3 into *practice* (see Section 2.3.1 for instructions).
   - Second, the variables "homework," "practice," and "grade" do not have a detailed description yet. Define in **Label** what the variables represent (see Section 2.3.2 for SPSS and page 14 for the definition of the variables).
   - Third, the variables "sex," "study," "homework," and "enroll" do not have value labels (see Section 2.3.3 for SPSS and pages 23–24 for the exact value labels). Add these to the file.
   - Switch to *Data View*, and, if necessary, go to **View** in the menu bar (see instructions on page 21) and switch **value labels** on, to check whether the value labels have been entered correctly.
   - Finally, the file contains the information of 37 students. The data of the three remaining students have not yet been entered. Add them to the file in the empty rows directly beneath the last respondent (see Section 2.3.5). The remaining three students have the following scores on the variables:

respnr	age	sex	study	enroll	homework
6	18	0	0	0	33
9	30	0	0	1	24
40	36	1	1	1	32

compu1	compu2	compu3	practice	theory	grade
3	1	2	2	3	7.3[a]
2	4	4	5	5	6.2
4	4	3	3	4	7.5

a. Because of the language settings other than English in the Windows control panel, your computer may accept a comma and not a dot.

3. The data file is now ready except for one issue. A number of students did not answer some of the questions. In our data file, students who did not provide answers to specific questions received the value 999. Now this value will still be included in the SPSS calculations. To prevent this from happening, we define it as "missing values" (when not defined thus, SPSS would, for instance, calculate an absurdly high average for the variable "homework"). So define 999 as a missing value for the variable "homework" (see Section 2.3.4).

4. To check whether 999 indeed is a missing value, you may look at the frequency distribution of the variable "homework." You can create this distribution yourself by using the menu bar. Click on **Analyze, Descriptives Statistics ▶ Frequencies . . .** Then, double-click on "homework" and finally click **OK**. (We will discuss frequency tables in detail in Chapter 4; for reference, Figure 4.1 on page 51 may suffice here).

5. Look in the output window (see Section 1.5.2) for the frequency table that shows the distribution of "homework" (if necessary, activate this window via **Window** in the menu bar). Verify the following: Students spent between 15 and 41 minutes on statistics homework. Note that the four students with score 999 are no longer part of the "valid" observations as indicated by the differences between "percent" and "valid percent."

6. Now save the adapted data file fictitious.sav. Make sure to give it a different name: *chapter2fictitious* (preferably store it in the **SPSS**

Basics folder). If the data file is given a new name, the original file is retained, which allows the user to return to the original data in case of a computer malfunction or incorrect changes.

- Save the contents of the output window (i.e., frequency distributions of "age," "homework," and "study") as *outputchapter2* (see Section 2.5 for information on how to save files).

7. Check to see whether all files have actually been saved (see Section 2.2). If everything has been saved with correct names, then you may continue with the next chapter or close SPSS by clicking on the ⊠ icon in the top right-hand side of each window. You do not have to save any more files as you have already done so in Assignment 6. Please do not overwrite any files created in this chapter or in the remaining chapters. You can prevent over-writing by giving the file a new, unique name when saved.

Chapter 3
Data Modifications

3.1 Introduction △

Editing or modifying variables is known as *data modification*. Although the term *modification* might sound a bit like manipulating data, this is not the case. Sometimes the data in SPSS cannot be directly used for statistical analyses or variables do not correspond to the ones the researcher wishes to use. Data modification in this chapter simply means the transformation or adaptation of data to make it fit for statistical applications. There are various ways to do this. For example,

- recoding existing variables,
- computing new variables,
- selecting cases from a data file, or
- splitting the data file into groups.

Selecting cases and splitting a file are, strictly speaking, not part of the data modification process but belong to file modification. They are, however, covered in this chapter as they, like data modification, still constitute key steps that precede descriptive and inferential statistical analysis (discussed in Chapters 4 and 5).

3.2 Recode Variables △

Variables are recoded for two reasons, namely,

1. to modify certain values of a variable and
2. to group certain values into one single value.

In recoding, there are two options, namely,

1. recode into same variables or
2. recode into different variables.

3.2.1 Recode Into Same Variables

With this command, the variable keeps the same name and labels, with the new (recoded) values in the same column. As a consequence, the original data are overwritten and lost! There is no way to control the process and no way to undo the action save returning to the original file. Therefore, you are advised not to use this method of recoding!

3.2.2 Recode Into Different Variables

This method retains the original variable, which, of course, is very often exactly what a user wants. The values are added to the file under a new variable name in the first empty column of the data file.

Example

Let us assume that someone wants to know whether there is a difference between the level of computer skills of younger and older students. The values of the "age" variable must then first be recoded into the categories "young" (younger students, i.e., between 18 and 28 years of age) and "older" (older students, i.e., between 29 and 37 years of age).

The "Recode into Same Variables" option is not useful here as the original variable "age" is important and must be retained. The following instructions are part of "Recode into Different Variables."

- If not already open, start SPSS.
- First go to **Edit**, then to **Options**..., and, if necessary, check **Display names** (directly under the **General** tab) and click **OK**. Click **OK** again after you receive a notification of the change (from now on you will be able to see the variable names in the dialog window instead of the labels).
- Open the file *chapter3fictitious.sav*.

If the output window appears instead of the data window, then
- Go to **Window** in the menu bar and then click on *chapter3fictitious.sav* to activate the data window.

- In the menu bar, select   Transform
                                Recode into Different Variables...

The dialog window "Recode into Different Variables" now opens (Figure 3.1).

Figure 3.1   Dialog Window "Recode into Different Variables"

- Double-click on the variable to be recoded (in this case, "age"), thereby placing it in the box (see Figure 3.1).
- Click on the box directly beneath **Name** and fill in a name for the new variable. Use *youngold* as the new name (see Figure 3.1).
- Then, click on **Change**.

Now the values of the new variable must be defined. In this case, we need to indicate which values of the original variable "age" correspond to the new categories "young" and "old."

Click **Old and New Values**.

The dialog window "Recode into Different Variables: Old and New Values" will open:

Figure 3.2 "Recode into Different Variables: Old and New Values"

- Check **Range** in the **Old Value** section (see Figure 3.2) by clicking the small circle in front of **Range**. Recode the age range 18 to 28 years by clicking on the empty box above *through* and type 18. Then, click on the empty box beneath *through* and type 28 (see Figure 3.2, Old Value, Range).
- In the **New Value** section, click on the empty box right of *Value* and type 1 (see Figure 3.2, New Value).
- Click **Add** (recoding will appear in the Old → New: box).
- Repeat the procedure for age 29 to 37 years who receive the new value 2 (see Figure 3.2, Old → New:).

The recoding of the variable "age" into "youngold" is complete:

Click on **Continue**.

The dialog window "Recode into Different Variables" (Figure 3.1) will then reappear.

- Click **OK** in the window to execute the recoding.
- If needed, switch to *chapter3fictitious.sav*.
- Select Variable View and provide names for the two values of the "youngold" variable: 1 = "young" and 2 = "old" (see Section 2.3.3). The new variable is then ready for use.

3.3 Create New Variables △

SPSS provides the option to create new variables from a combination of other existing variables.

Example

In the data file, we have several indicators of computer skills. If we are interested in knowing the general level of computer skills of all the students in the study, we must add up all the variables that measured computer skills. In this example, we have three questions (also known as indicators, variables, or items): "compu1" (word processing), "compu2" (spreadsheets), and "compu3" (Windows). As the variables "compu1," "compu2," and "compu3" have values that range from 1 (very poor skills) up to 5 (very good skills), the new variable may run from a minimum of 3 (poorest skills) to a maximum of 15 (highest skills).

Note that strictly speaking the variables "compu1," "compu2," and "compu3" are measured on an ordinal scale. For instance, we know that the category "very poor skills" (coded 1) is below "poor skills" (coded 2), but we do not know exactly how low. Addition of scores would therefore make little sense. In this case, however, we treat them as variables with interval scales (i.e., assuming that the difference between subsequent categories is always 1, which is the common practice in research. The resulting variable is often called a Likert (pronounced "lick-urt") scale.

In the menu bar, click   **Transform**
                                Compute Variable . . .

The dialog window "Compute Variable" will appear; see Figure 3.3.

Figure 3.3 Dialog Window "Compute Variable"

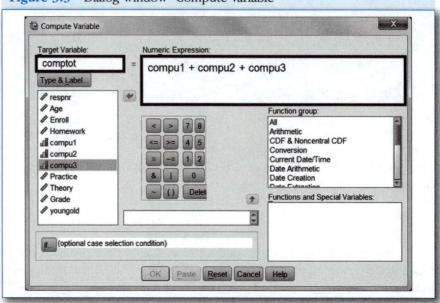

Enter the name of the target variable to be calculated ("comptot") into the empty box located directly beneath **Target Variable** (see Figure 3.3).

Like in recoding, we recommend to give the new variable a different name, so that no existing variable is overwritten in the process. The computation has to be entered into the **Numeric Expression** box of the "Compute Variable" dialog window (see Figure 3.3). You will be able to enter an arithmetic operation directly into the box or select it with the cursor. In this example, we need to *add* the values of all three variables measuring computer skills:

- Select the **Numeric Expression** box and enter *compu1 + compu2 + compu3* (see Figure 3.3).
- Then, click on   OK.

The calculation for "comptot" is now complete, and this new variable is added to the data file (see Figure 3.4). For a final check, you may verify that the values for "comptot" are indeed the sum of "compu1," "compu2," and "compu3."

Figure 3.4 Data Window: Variable "comptot" Added

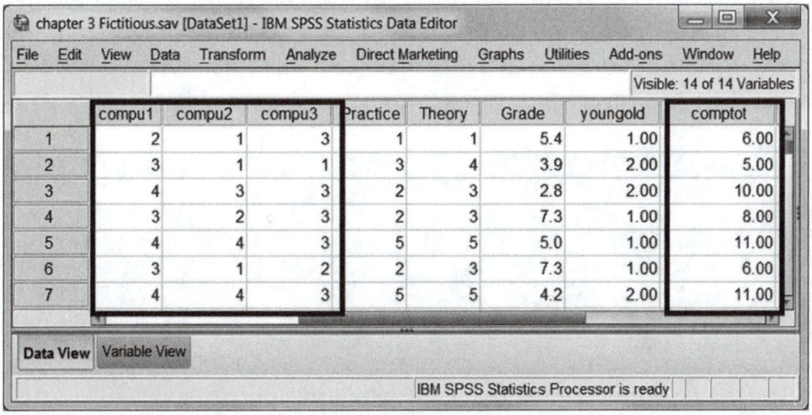

You may provide a more detailed description of the variable "comptot." Add, for instance, "computer skills total" in **Label** that is part of the Variable View window (see Figure 3.5). See the relevant instructions in Section 2.3.2: "Add Variable Labels."

Figure 3.5 Data Window: Variable "comptot" Added

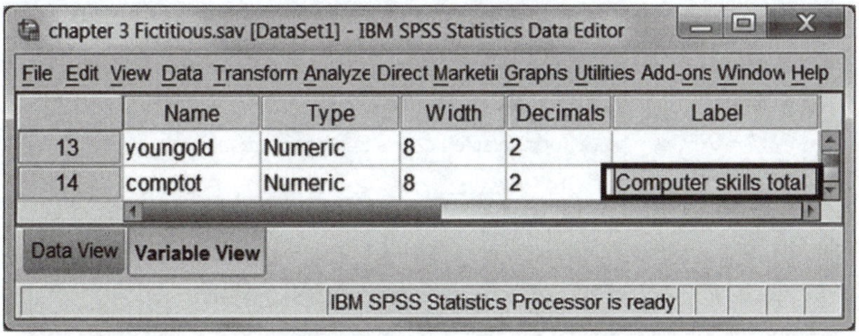

△ 3.4 Select Cases

It is quite common to run statistical analyses on only a selected subset of the respondents (cases) in the data file.

Example

Say, a researcher is only interested in the evaluation results of students who are enrolled only full-time, while the file contains all students—both part-time and full-time. In such a scenario, all full-time students need to be selected first (i.e., everyone with a 0 value for the variable "enroll").

In the menu bar, go to   **Data**
                              Select Cases . . .

The dialog window "Select Cases" will now appear (see Figure 3.6):

Figure 3.6   Dialog Window "Select Cases"

Select Cases

Select
- ○ All cases
- ◉ If condition is satisfied
  - [If...]
- ○ Random sample of cases
  - [Sample...]
- ○ Based on time or case range
  - [Range...]
- ○ Use filter variable:

Variables:
- respnr
- Age
- sex
- Study
- Enroll
- Homework
- compu1
- compu2
- compu3
- Practice
- Theory
- Grade
- youngold
- comptot

Output
- ◉ Filter out unselected cases
- ○ Copy selected cases to a new dataset
  - Dataset name: [ ]

Current Status: Do not filter cases

[OK] [Paste] [Reset] [Cancel] [Help]

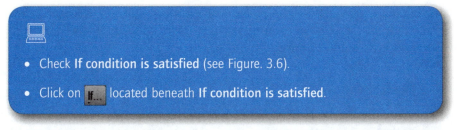

- Check **If condition is satisfied** (see Figure. 3.6).

- Click on **If...** located beneath **If condition is satisfied**.

The dialog window "Select Cases: If" will now appear (see Figure 3.7):

Figure 3.7 Dialog Window "Select Cases If"

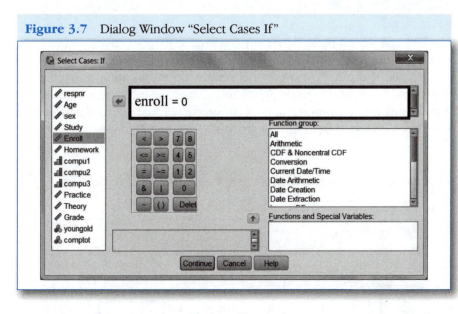

In this window, you are able to indicate that we are interested only in full-time students. This means that only students with value 0 (full-time) on the variable "enroll" have to be selected.

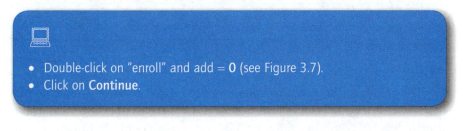

- Double-click on "enroll" and add = **0** (see Figure 3.7).
- Click on **Continue**.

The "Select Cases" window returns after this operation. In the dialog window, just below **Output**, you will find the option "Filter out unselected cases" checked (see Figure 3.6). This means that only full-time students (the students who have the value 0 for the variable "enroll") will be included in any analysis to come while others will be excluded. This excluded list of part-time students, however, still has to be executed before it is actually effective.

Click on   OK.

The task is complete now: *only* full-time students (value 0) have been selected. After returning to the Data View window (if needed switch to **Data View** if the Variable View window is active), the notification "Filter On" in the status bar in the bottom right-hand corner is visible (see Figure 3.8). This means that part-time students (the rows marked with a dash) indeed have been excluded from further analysis (again see Figure 3.8).

Figure 3.8   Data Window: Data View (active) and Full-Time Students Selected

respnr	Age	Sex	Study	Enroll	Homework
1	1	21	.00	.00	0	999
2	2	32	1.00	1.00	1	15
3	3	29	.00	1.00	1	24
4	4	21	.00	.00	0	36

*chapter 3 Fictitious.sav [DataSet1] - IBM SPSS Statistics Data Editor

File   Edit   View   Data   Transform   Analyze   Direct Marketing   Graphs   Utilities   Add-ons   Window   Help

Visible: 15 of 15 Variables

Data View   Variable View

Processor area   IBM SPSS Statistics Processor is ready   Filter On

Selection effective

The analyses that will subsequently be executed now only relate to students who are enrolled full-time. For instance, we like to know the average (mean) level of computer skills for full-time students only. In Chapter 4, the use of statistical measures like the mean is more extensively covered. Here, we use it only to show the potential of "Select Cases."

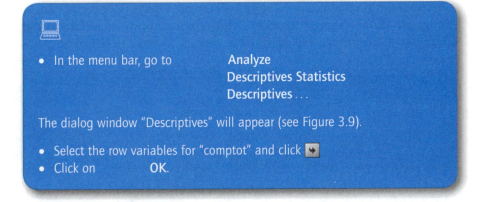

- In the menu bar, go to

  Analyze
  Descriptives Statistics
  Descriptives . . .

The dialog window "Descriptives" will appear (see Figure 3.9).

- Select the row variables for "comptot" and click ➡
- Click on **OK**.

Check the results to find (see Table 3.1) if the average level of computer skills of full-time students (in this case, 7.5556) has been calculated correctly in your case.

Figure 3.9 Dialog Window "Descriptives"

Table 3.1 The Average Level of Computer Skills for Full-Time Students

	N	Minimum	Maximum	Mean	Std. Deviation
comptot	18	6.00	11.00	7.5556	1.61690

The selection that has been made will remain effective for further applications. The following applications in this chapter, however, relate to the entire file (all students), which is why we need to undo the selection:

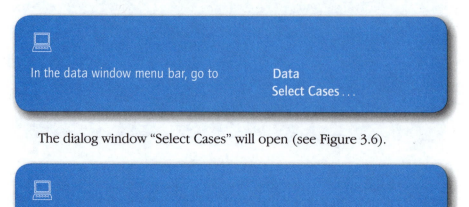

In the data window menu bar, go to   **Data**
         Select Cases . . .

The dialog window "Select Cases" will open (see Figure 3.6).

- Check   **All cases**.
- Click   **OK**.

The selection of full-time students is undone, and the dashes through the respondent numbers in the data window disappear, while "Filter On" no longer shows up in the status bar.

△ 3.5 Split Files

In general, statistical analyses are done on several groups separately, for this the data need to be split up.

Example

Assume that you want to find the average level of computer skills for male and female students separately. Using the "Split File," respondents are split into groups, based on one (or more) variable(s), after which analyses can be run on each group separately.

In the data window menu bar, go to   **Data**
         Split File . . .

The dialog window "Split File" will appear:

Figure 3.10 Dialog Window "Split File"

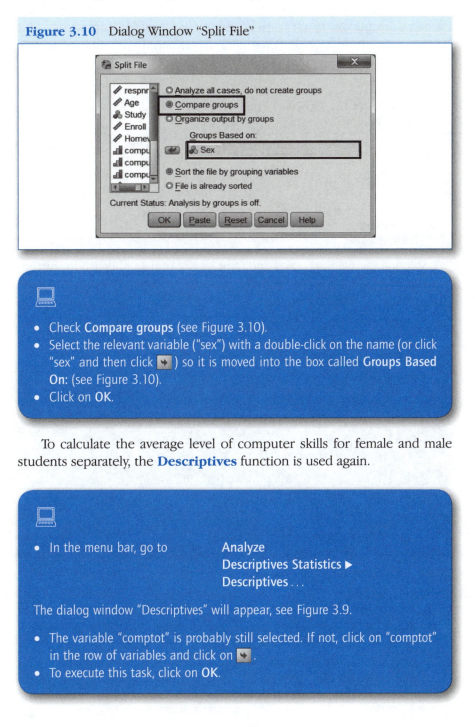

- Check **Compare groups** (see Figure 3.10).
- Select the relevant variable ("sex") with a double-click on the name (or click "sex" and then click ➡) so it is moved into the box called **Groups Based On:** (see Figure 3.10).
- Click on **OK**.

To calculate the average level of computer skills for female and male students separately, the **Descriptives** function is used again.

- In the menu bar, go to   Analyze
                                      Descriptives Statistics ▶
                                      Descriptives . . .

The dialog window "Descriptives" will appear, see Figure 3.9.

- The variable "comptot" is probably still selected. If not, click on "comptot" in the row of variables and click on ➡ .
- To execute this task, click on **OK**.

Once the instructions have been followed correctly, the mean values of the variable "comptot" will appear in the output window (see Table 3.2). From this table, it is clear that the mean level of computer skills among male students is lower (7.7857) compared with that of female students (8.6154).

Table 3.2 Mean Values for the Variable "comptot" (computer skills total) for Female and Male Students Separately

Sex		N	Minimum	Maximum	Mean	Std. Deviation
0 Male	comptot	14	6.00	11.00	7.7857	1.76193
	Valid N (listwise)	14				
1 Female	comptot	26	5.00	11.00	8.6154	2.02142
	Valid N (listwise)	26				

Splitting the file into males and females will remain effective for further analysis. However, for the assignments in the next section this is not needed. It is possible to undo the split by checking the option **Analyze all cases, do no create groups** in the "Split File" dialog window as follows:

- Go to the data window (via **Window** in the main menu and select *chapter3-fictitious*).
- In the menu bar, go to
  - Data
  - Split File . . .
- Select **Analyze, all cases, do not create groups** and click **OK**.
- To check, calculate the mean level of computer skills again (via **Analyze, descriptive statistics ▶ descriptives** . . . , see page 43) and check whether the mean for all (40) the students is 8.325.

△ 3.6 Assignments

1. Someone wants to know the average number of lectures attended by part-time students. One way to obtain this information is to only select part-time students (see Section 3.4) and to subsequently let SPSS calculate the mean of the variable "theory." Follow the steps you

learned in this chapter to find this mean value. In the "Descriptives" dialog window, you can remove the variable "comptot" by selecting the variable and click on ⬅).

2. Undo the selection of only part-time students (Section 3.4).

3. Calculate the means for the variable "comptot" (computer skills total) separately for younger and older students (see Section 3.5). Use the new variable "youngold" with its categories of young and old (see Section 3.2) instead of the original variable "age." Make sure to remove the variable "sex" from the box "Groups based on" (select the variable and click ⬅).

4. Is the mean level of computer skills among younger students higher or lower compared with the average among older students?

5. Undo the split in young and old students (see end of Section 3.5).

6. Save all SPSS results from this chapter as an output file named *outputchapter3* and save the data file under the (new) name *chapter3-new* (preferably, both files are saved in the folder **SPSS Basics**).

7. Before continuing please check that both files are saved by using a file explorer program like Windows Explorer (🗔). If the files are saved, then close the output window *outputchapter3* (also close other active output windows if there are any). If you like to continue with Chapter 4 in this session, then leave the data window open. SPSS will continue to be active.

Chapter 4
Descriptive Statistics

In Chapter 1, we stressed the importance of statistical programs like SPSS in the research process. In Chapters 2 and 3, we explained how data can be entered into the data files of SPSS and can be modified further. In this chapter (as well as in Chapter 5), we cover the actual statistical analysis of the data.

Before statistical tests are performed (see Chapter 5), a thorough description is necessary. Descriptive statistics can be very useful to gain insight into the variables at hand (for instance, see Figure 1.3). In addition, it allows you to check not only whether the data have been correctly entered but also whether the data can be used for statistical purposes. It also helps calculate well-known statistical measures such as the mean. Most descriptive procedures in SPSS are listed in "**Descriptive Statistics**," a submenu within the main menu "**Analyze**." The four main commands are (1) **Frequencies**, (2) **Descriptives**, (3) **Explore**, and (4) **Crosstabs**:

1. **Frequencies:** The Frequencies command is used to retrieve frequency distributions. In other words, to determine the popularity of occurring values in absolute numbers and percentages. In addition, the frequency distribution can be displayed in graphs.

2. **Descriptives:** The Descriptives command is used to calculate statistical measures such as the mean (in Sections 3.4 and 3.5). Note that most measures that are calculated with this command are only useful in cases where the distance between the successive values of a variable is known. The "age" variable is a good example for this: The distance between 10 and 20 years old is exactly 50% of the distance between 30 and 50 years old. Such variables are called quantitative variables or ratio/interval scaled variables. Results are displayed in a more clear and concise table than in Frequencies, but Descriptives cannot be used to create diagrams or charts.

3. **Explore:** This command is used in extensive analysis of variables. In addition to many common statistical measures, the frequency distribution can be shown in histograms and/or boxplots. Division into groups and comparison of frequency distributions within those groups is also possible, enabling in-depth analysis.

4. **Crosstabs:** The Crosstabs command allows for a variety of measures of association using cross-tables. In general, these tables are used for qualitative variables. There are two types of qualitative variables: (1) ordinal variables and (2) nominal variables. Ordinal variables have values or categories with a certain rank order. The exact distances between adjacent categories, however, are not known (not quantifiable). Consider the variable "education": Elementary school is at the lowest level, university is the highest level, and senior high school is somewhere in between, but it is difficult to locate where exactly. In nominal variables, a rank order is not possible. Consider the variable "marital status": Married people are not "higher" ranked than single people. The values assigned to categories such as "married" and "single" are thus arbitrary and serve only to differentiate between categories. We address the analyses of cross-tables also in Chapter 5, where we introduce statistical testing.

△ 4.2 Frequency Tables

A frequency table shows the frequency of occurrence for every category. This can be done with absolute numbers but more common are percentages.

Example

Suppose you want to know the frequency distribution of the number of practice sessions attended.

- If you have not already done so, start SPSS.
- Open the file *chapter4fictitious.sav*.
- Via Edit → check to see if Display names is on (see instructions in the box on page 34).
- In the data window menu bar, click on

  Analyze
  Descriptives Statistics ▶ Frequencies . . .

The dialog window "Frequencies" will open (see Figure 4.1). In this window, you can indicate from which variable(s) you want a frequency table by placing the variable in the **Variable(s)** box:

From the list of variables, click "practice" and click on ⬛ (but do not click **OK**).

Figure 4.1 Dialog Window "Frequencies"

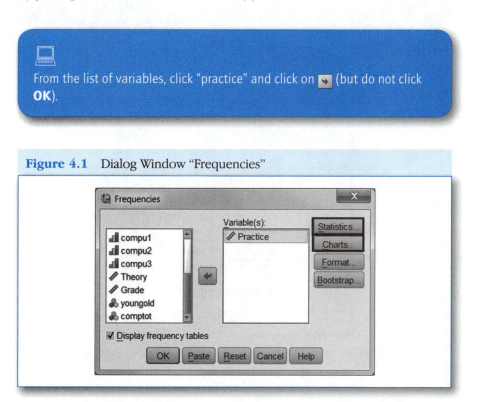

Besides a frequency table, we can also retrieve statistical measures for the "practice" variable:

Click on   **Statistics**.

The dialog window "Frequencies: Statistics" will show up (see Figure 4.2). In this window, you may indicate which descriptive statistical measures you wish to calculate. We have opted to calculate mean, median, mode, standard deviation, range, minimum, and maximum. The instructions to achieve this are as follows:

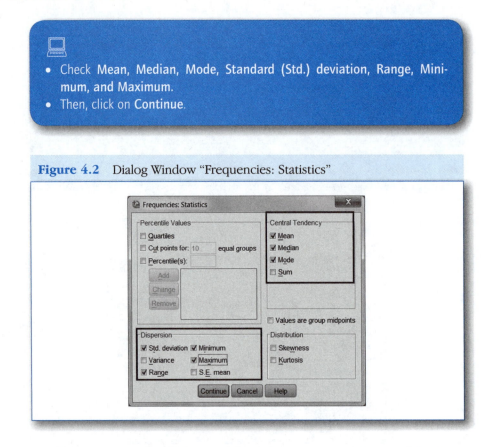

- Check **Mean, Median, Mode, Standard (Std.) deviation, Range, Minimum, and Maximum.**
- Then, click on **Continue**.

Figure 4.2 Dialog Window "Frequencies: Statistics"

This reopens the dialog window "Frequencies" (Figure 4.1). Now you can indicate the charts that are to be included after the statistical measures.

Click on   **Charts**.

The dialog window "Frequencies: Charts" opens (see Figure 4.3).

In this window, bar charts and histograms can be created. The number of practice sessions is a quantitative variable, so a histogram is the best chart (if the variable had been qualitative, i.e., ordinal or nominal, then a bar chart would be appropriate).

Figure 4.3 Dialog Window "Frequencies: Charts"

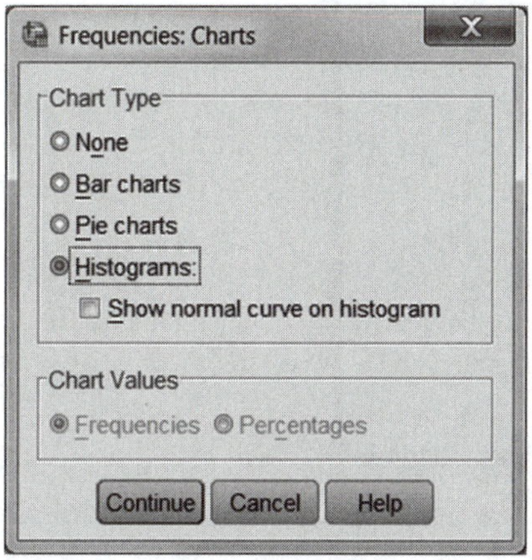

Check **Histograms** and click on **Continue**.

The "Frequencies" dialog window reopens:

Click on **OK**.

The following results are to be found in the output window, see Table 4.1 and Figure 4.4.

4.3 Pie Charts △

In statistics, as in life, a picture is sometimes worth a thousand words. Graphs provide a great deal of insight into the distribution of a variable. In addition, charts are very useful tools for clearly and concisely representing

Table 4.1 Statistics and Frequency Distribution of the Variable "practice"

N	40
Mean	3.90
Median	4.00
Mode	4
Std. Deviation	−1.008
Range	4
Minimum	1
Maximum	5

		Frequency	Percent	Valid Percent	Cumulative Percent
Valid	1.00	1	2.5	2.5	2.5
	2.00	3	7.5	7.5	10.0
	3.00	7	17.5	17.5	27.5
	4.00	17	42.5	42.5	70.0
	5.00	12	30.0	30.0	100.0
	Total	40	100.0	100.0	

research findings. Therefore, a key function in the SPSS package is its ability to create charts.

The **Graphs** menu can generate a great variety of graphs. In addition, the menu option **Analyze** (and then **Descriptive Statistics → Frequencies**) can be used to create histograms and bar charts (see the previous section).

Example

The results for the variable "compu1" (word processing skills) can be represented in a pie chart as follows:

- In the menu bar, click **Graphs, Legacy dialogs** . . . (see Figure 4.5).
- Point at **Pie** . . . in the menu, and click after it highlights (see Figure 4.5).

Figure 4.4 Histogram for the Variable "practice"

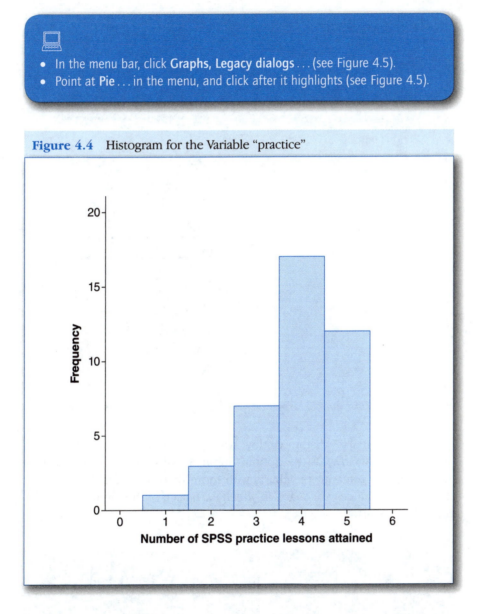

Note that in the "Legacy Dialogs" there is a large variety of graphs to choose from. Bar (chart), line, pie (chart), boxplot, scatter (plot), and histogram are widely used.

Figure 4.5 Dialog Window "Legacy Dialogs"

Graphs	Utilities	Add-ons	Window	Help

- 📊 Chart Builder...
- 🖼 Graphboard Template Chooser...
- 📦 R Boxplot...
- Legacy Dialogs ▸

Legacy Dialogs submenu:
- 📊 Bar...
- 📊 3-D Bar...
- 📈 Line...
- 📊 Area...
- 🥧 Pie...
- 📊 High-Low...
- 📊 Boxplot...
- 📊 Error Bar...
- 📊 Population Pyramid...
- 📊 Scatter/Dot...
- 📊 Histogram...

The "Pie Charts" dialog window will appear (Figure 4.6). The default setting of this window is the option "Summaries for groups of cases" (the second option refers to pie charts with more than one variable, while the last option produces pie charts in which each slice of the pie represents an individual score).

Click on   Define.

The dialog window "Define Pie: Summaries for groups of cases" will open (Figure 4.7).

In this window, you may indicate which variable is to be presented in a pie chart (in this case, it is the variable "compu1" [word processing skills]).

Figure 4.6   Dialog Window "Pie Charts"

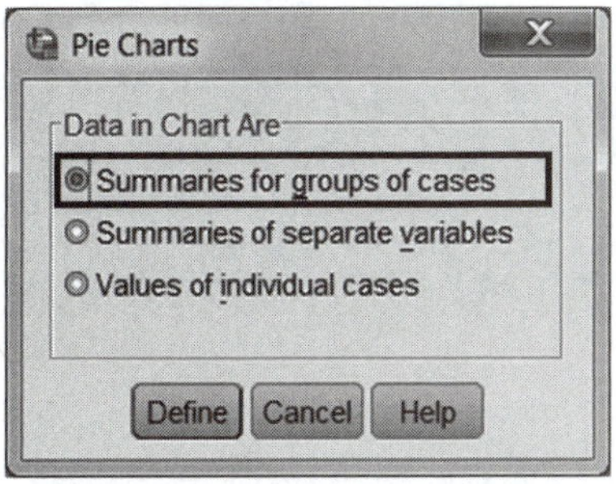

Figure 4.7   Dialog Window "Define Pie: Summaries for Groups of Cases"

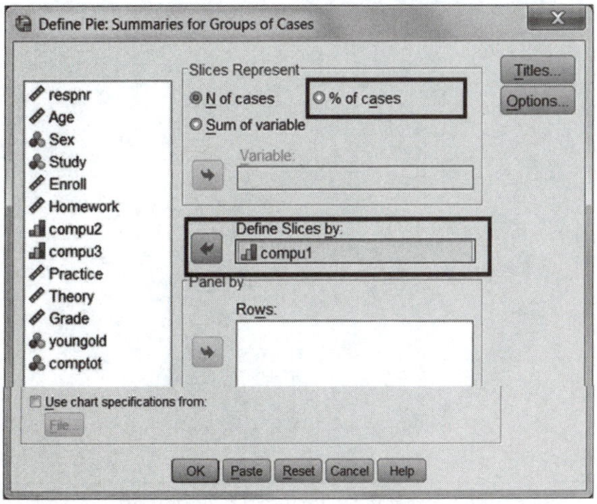

- Click on "compu1" and then click ➡ (in front of the **Define Slices by** box; see Figure 4.7).
- Check **% of cases** (this will enable the percentages to show later).
- Click on **OK**.

This will generate a pie chart that represents the variable "compu1" (see Figure 4.8). The pie chart can be modified by the user as follows:

Double-click on the pie chart located in the output window.

Figure 4.8   Pie Chart "compu1"

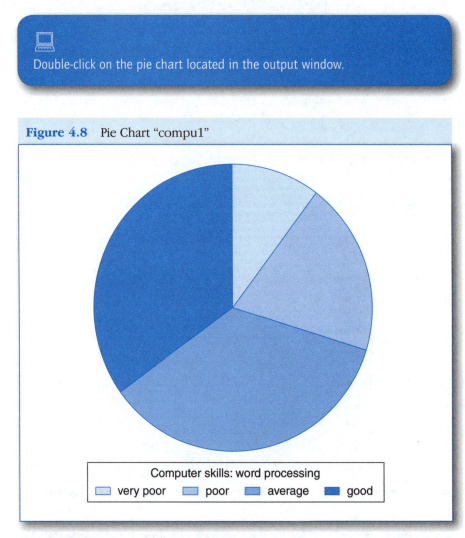

Note: "compu1": computer skills in word processing.

Like any other chart in SPSS, the pie chart will now be loaded in a so-called chart editor and can be modified. The chart editor has its own menu bar (see Figure 4.9). This menu bar contains six drop-down menus: (1) File, (2) Edit, (3) View, (4) Options, (5) Elements, and (6) Help. We briefly describe these menus:

1. *File:* In this menu, you can save your settings (templates) or apply other (previously saved) settings. There is also an option for exporting charts to XML format.
2. *Edit:* The most important feature in this menu is "Properties," which contains options for styles, titles, legends, and boxes.
3. *View:* This is to indicate which toolbars are to be visible in the editor.
4. *Options:* This menu is for adding additional features to your charts.
5. *Elements:* In this menu, labels are added, as well as linear regression lines (in scatterplots).
6. *Help:* This menu contains references to SPSS help functions to generate charts.

In the chart editor menu bar, click on the following:
Elements → **Show data labels** (see Figure 4.9) and click on **close** in the dialog window "Properties" that was opened.

Figure 4.9   Chart Editor

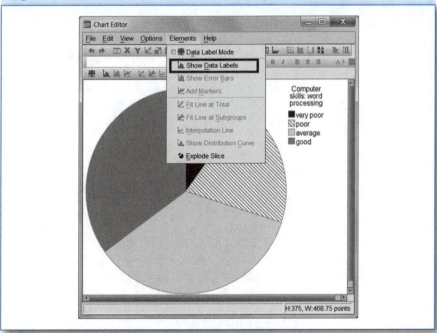

Note: Pie chart with "compu1."

The pie chart will also display the percentages (this was the reason for checking **% of cases**, see Figure 4.7). Visually, it is much easier to compare the length (as in a bar chart or a histogram) than an area (as in a pie chart). That is why percentages should be listed in a pie chart to avoid any misconception.

Once you close the editor (by clicking ⊠ at the top right-hand corner of the window), the modified chart (with %) will be shown in the output window.

△ 4.4 Boxplots

Boxplots are graphs that are tailor-made for comparing the distribution of a (at least ordinal) variable in various groups.

In the menu bar, click on   **Graphs**
                                     Legacy dialogs ▶ Boxplot...

The dialog window "Boxplot" (Figure 4.10) will appear and is already set to "Simple" ("Clustered" is used for multiple variables).

Figure 4.10   Dialog Window "Boxplot"

Click on **Define**.

The dialog window "Define Simple Boxplot" will open in which one can enter the variables to generate the boxplot:

- Place the variable "homework" in the Variable box (click on the variable name and then click on ➡).
- Place the variable "study" in the Category Axis box (see Figure 4.11).
- Click on **OK**.

Figure 4.11 Dialog Window "Define Simple Boxplot"

> **Define Simple Boxplot: Summaries for Groups of Cases**   ✕
>
> - respnr
> - Age
> - Sex
> - Enroll
> - compu1
> - compu2
> - compu3
> - Practice
> - Theory
>
> Variable:
> ➡ *Homework*
>
> Category Axis:
> ➡ Study
>
> Label Cases by :
> ➡
>
> Panel by
> Rows:
> ▪ Nest variables (no empty columns)
>
> OK   Paste   Reset   Cancel   Help
>
> Options...

The boxplots will now be displayed in the output window (see Figure 4.12).

Figure 4.12 Boxplot With "homework"

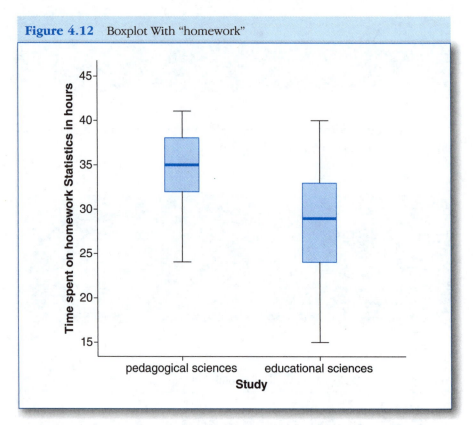

Note: Hours spent on statistics assignments among students in pedagogical and educational sciences.

The median (the bold line in the gray boxes in Figure 4.12) indicates that pedagogical science students generally spent more time doing statistics than educational science students did. The height of the blue-shaded rectangles indicates the difference between the minimum and maximum scores of the middle 50% of all observations. This difference is called the *interquartile range* and is a measure of the variation in time spent on statistics. This variation is smallest among pedagogical science students.

▵ 4.5 Graphs With Chart Builder

After the classical graphs, SPSS introduced the *chart builder*, for advanced applications. We briefly describe this as the menu has many options available.

Example

One may want to show the relationship between homework and the final grade in statistics. Because both variables are quantitative, we may use a scatterplot or a line graph. Because the latter shows the trend more clearly, we explain how to create such a graph.

In the menu bar, click on **Graphs**, **Legacy dialog**s … ▶ **chart builder** (see Figure 4.5).

Depending on the settings on your computer, you may first see a message (see Figure 4.13). Click on **OK** as the variables are defined correctly.

Figure 4.13   Chart Builder's Message About Measurement Levels

- Click on "Line" in the "**Choose from**" box (see Figure 4.14).
- Double-click on the single-line box next to "Line."
- Click on "homework," and drag it to *x*-axis (keep the left mouse button pressed as you move across the menu and release [drop] it just below the *x*-axis).
- Drag and drop the variable "grade" on *y*-axis.
- Click **OK** (for detailed results see Figure 4.15).

Figure 4.14 Dialog Window "Chart Builder"

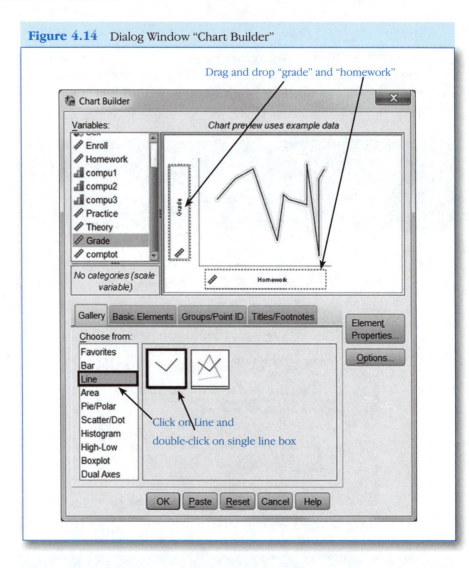

△ 4.6 Contingency Tables

Cross-tables are perfect for often—ordinal or nominal—variables that do not have too many different values. This means that variables should have a limited number of categories as most qualitative variables have.

In bivariate tables, two variables are cross-tabled. Using percentile differences and/or measures of association, such as Cramér's V (based on chi-square [χ^2]) and Kendall's tau, we can determine whether there is a statistical relationship between the two variables and how strong the relationship is.

Figure 4.15 Line Graph of Mean Score Per Hour of Homework (positive trend)

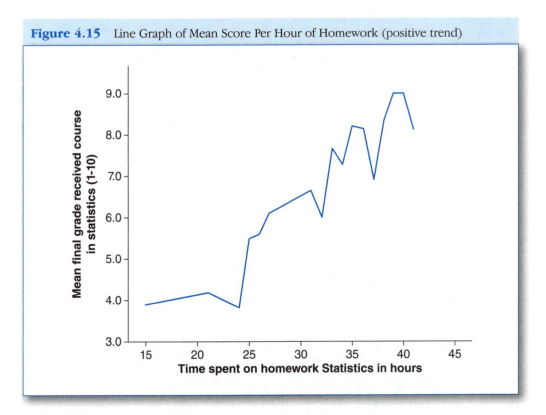

Example

Suppose someone wants to know whether there is a relationship between gender and field of study.

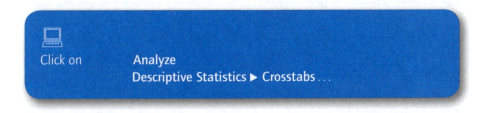

Click on   Analyze
                  Descriptive Statistics ▶ Crosstabs . . .

The dialog window "Crosstabs" will open (see Figure 4.16). To create a simple cross-table, all you need to do is provide variables for the row and column, and then click on **OK**. Generally, the independent variable is placed in columns and the dependent variable in rows. However, you may change if the table does not fit the page.

Figure 4.16 Dialog Window "Crosstabs"

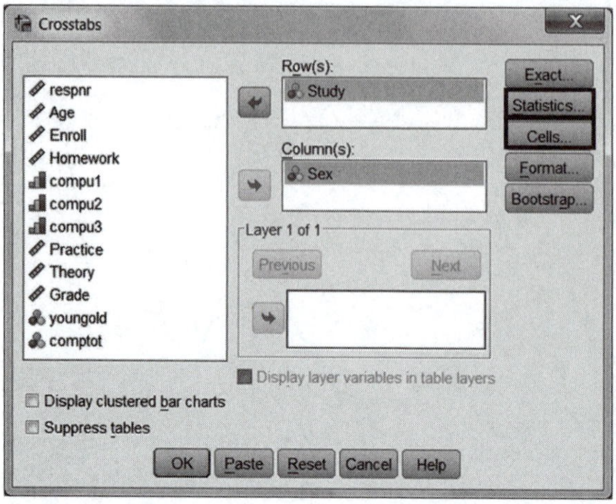

- Place "study" in the rows (**Row(s)**) and "sex" in the columns (**Column(s)**) by clicking on the names and then on ➡ (see Figure 4.16).
- Then, click on **OK**.

The result is a cross-table that contains the absolute numbers of men and women who study pedagogical and educational sciences (see Table 4.2). Cross-tables will always display the absolute numbers by default. The table shows that the number of females who choose pedagogical sciences (13) is almost equal to the number of males who did so (12). This does not mean, however, that women and men have an almost equal preference for pedagogical sciences, given that the total number of women (26) is not equal to the total number of men (14).

Using the **Cells** option in the "Crosstabs" dialog window, you may modify or expand the content of the cells, for example, calculate percentages to take into account the difference between the total number of women and total number of men. In the "Crosstabs: Cell Display" window, you can select the information you like to present in a cross-table.

Table 4.2 Results for "Crosstabs"

		Sex		
		.00 Male	**1.00 Female**	**Total**
Study	.00 Pedagogical sciences	12	13	25
	1.00 Educational sciences	2	13	15
Total		14	26	40

- Again go to **Analyze**, **Descriptive Statistics** ▶ and to **Crosstabs**.
- In the "Crosstabs" window, click on **Cells**.

The "Crosstabs: Cell Display" dialog window will appear (see Figure 4.17; the less relevant "Noninteger Weights" option is not shown here).

Figure 4.17 Dialog Window "Crosstabs: Cell Display"

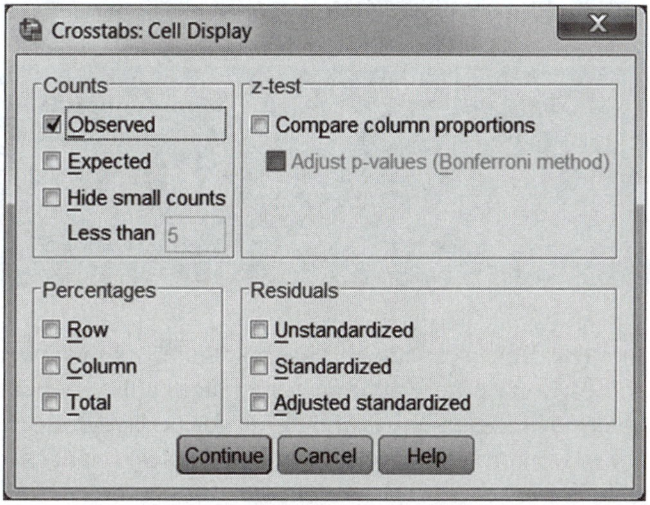

In this window (Figure 4.17), the content of the cells can be adapted. There are three main options:

Counts

- *Observed:* observed frequencies (standard)
- *Expected:* expected frequencies under the condition that the variables have no statistical relationship

Percentages

- *Row:* row percentages, based on the row total
- *Column:* column percentages, based on the column total

Total: total percentages, based on the total number of observations

Residuals

- *Unstandardized:* the difference between the observed and the expected frequency (residual)
- *Standardized:* the residual divided by the root of the expected frequency
- *Adjusted standardized:* the residual is divided by its standard deviation

We follow the common practice of placing the independent variable in the columns and the dependent variable in the rows; percentages then must be based on the column totals:

- Figure 4.17, Check **Column**.
- Click on **Continue**.
- Click on **OK**.

The cross-table (see Table 4.3) has both numbers and column percentages. The comparison of these column percentages tells us whether women and men relatively have an equal preference for pedagogical sciences. The percentage of women who have chosen pedagogical sciences is 50 and is considerably lower than the percentage among men, which is 85.7. In conclusion, men choose pedagogical sciences over educational sciences relatively more often than women. We may also say that the probability of men to opt for pedagogical sciences is .857 and .5 for women. To gain

Table 4.3 Cross-Table With Numbers and Column Percentages

			Sex		Total
			.00 Male	**1.00 Female**	
Study	.00 Pedagogical sciences	Count	12	13	25
		Within sex (%)	85.7	50.0	62.5
	1.00 Educational sciences	Count	2	13	15
		Within sex (%)	14.3	50.0	37.5
Total		Count	14	26	40
		Within sex (%)	100.0	100.0	100.0

insight into the strength of the relationship between gender and study, we should calculate other measures of association. We will address this in detail in the next chapter.

For the cross-table analysis, we opted for a table with two columns and two rows, a so-called two-by-two (2 × 2) table. It is, however, perfectly possible to create a cross-table with different numbers of columns and/or rows, such as a three-by-two (3 × 2) table. If, for example, we had data on three fields of study, a table on the relationship between these three studies and sex would be appropriate. You can also use SPSS to create so-called trivariate tables, that is, cross-tables with three instead of two variables. Assume that you want to study the relationship between sex and study for various academic years. In order to carry out that study, the variable "academic year" (which we did not provide in our data set) must be added in the "Crosstabs" dialog window (Figure 4.16), in the **Layer 1 of 1** box.

4.7 Export to Word Processing Programs △

After results are generated and stored in the output file, you might like to export them to word processing programs, such as Microsoft Word, which is ideally suited for this. To include SPSS results in a text file, follow these instructions:

- Go to the output window (via **Windows** in the main menu), and click on the results to be included in a text file, for example, the table with variables "sex" and "study" (Table 4.3).
- In the menu bar, successively click on **Edit** and **Copy** (the table has now been copied).
- Open the word processing program, for example, Word.
- Move the cursor to the position on the page where the table should be located and simultaneously press the keys "Ctrl" and the letter "v." The table is copied into the file as a graph when using SPSS 21 or lower (see Table 4.4) and as a Word table in SPSS 22 (see Table 4.6).

Table 4.4   The Crosstabs Table Copied Into a Word File With Ctrl-c/v

Study * Sex Crosstabulation

			Sex		Total
			.00 male	1.00 female	
Study	.00 pedagogical sciences	Count	12	13	25
		% within Sex	85.7%	50.0%	62.5%
	1.00 educational sciences	Count	2	13	15
		% within Sex	14.3%	50.0%	37.5%
Total		Count	14	26	40
		% within Sex	100.0%	100.0%	100.0%

If you would like a real Word table that can be modified, click on the table in SPSS, then right click on the mouse and select **Export** and follow the instructions to save it as a .doc file. See Figure 4.18 for instructions and Tables 4.5 and 4.6 for results.

△ 4.8 Assignments

1. In most cases, the data file *chapter4fictitious.sav* may still be open. If not, open it again. Create a cross-table (see Section 4.5) from which you can infer to what extent younger students (aged 18 to 28 years) choose full-time over part-time enrollment more often than older students (aged 29 to 37 years) do. Use the variables "youngold" and

Table 4.5   The Export Menu to Copy a Crosstabs Table Copied Into a Word file

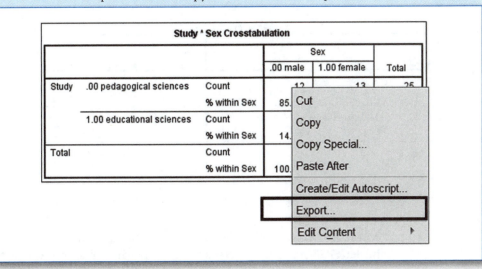

Figure 4.18   Dialog Window "Export Output"

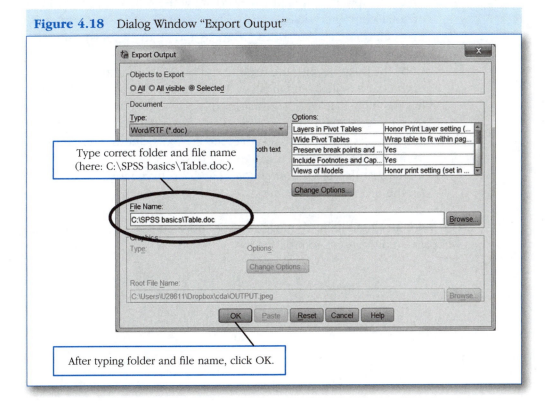

Table 4.6 The Crosstabs Table as a Real Word Table (file: Table.doc)

Study * Sex Crosstabulation

			Sex		
			.00 male	1.00 female	Total
Study	.00 pedagogical sciences	Count	12	13	25
		% within Sex	85.7%	50.0%	62.5%
	1.00 educational sciences	Count	2	13	15
		% within Sex	14.3%	50.0%	37.5%
Total		Count	14	26	40
		% within Sex	100.0%	100.0%	100.0%

"enroll." In "Crosstabs," indicate the correct percentage under "cells," and let SPSS retrieve the cross-table. Copy this table into a text file (e.g., a Word file) and add some text with some brief conclusions.

2. Create boxplots as in Figure 4.12 to show the difference in the level of total computer skills (variable "comptot" created in Chapter 3) between both age categories (18 to 28 and 29 to 37 years) using the variable "youngold."

3. Copy the boxplots into the text file and place it under the description of the cross-table from Question 1, and briefly describe which group has the highest level of computer skills.

4. Save the generated SPSS results as an output file. Name the file *outputchapter4*. Save the cross-table, the boxplots, and the descriptions in the text file as a file named *text*.

5. Check that the files *outputchapter4* and *text* have indeed been saved (in the **SPSS Basics** folder).

For more assignments in the field of descriptive statistics, please visit our webpage study.sagepub.com/basicspss.

Chapter 5
Inferential Statistics

5.1 Introduction △

In this chapter, we discuss some popular statistical tests, ranging from rather straightforward tests in cross-tables to more complex multivariate regression analysis. We could not help adding some basic information regarding statistical tests, but we kept it as brief as possible. This book emphasizes more on learning how to perform the tests in SPSS than to fully understand the underlying principles. To understand the principles, we refer the reader to *Discovering Statistics With SPSS* by Andy Field. The most important principle behind statistical testing is probability. In this chapter, we show that certain outcomes from samples, like a mean score, can be used to describe the target population from which the sample is drawn. This is what is meant by "statistical inference." The inference is done in terms of probability: Some values are more likely to exist in the population than others. By no means can statistical inference be used to prove something as being "true" or "false."

5.2 Associations in Contingency Tables △

In the previous chapter, we showed how cross-tables can be created. We now move on to some typical associations that are used in these tables. Again, we use the variables "gender" and "field of study."

Example

Suppose someone wants to know whether there is a relationship between gender and field of study.

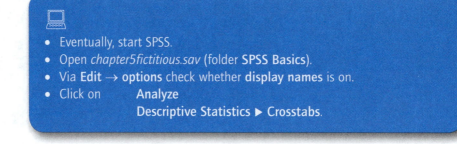

- Eventually, start SPSS.
- Open *chapter5fictitious.sav* (folder **SPSS Basics**).
- Via **Edit → options** check whether **display names** is on.
- Click on   **Analyze**
                Descriptive Statistics ▶ Crosstabs.

The dialog window "Crosstabs" will open (see Figure 4.16).

- Place "study" in the rows (**Row(s)**) and "sex" in the columns (**Column(s)**) by clicking on the names and then on ➡ (see Figure 4.16).
- In the "Crosstabs" window, click on **Cells**.

The "Crosstabs: Cell Display" dialog window will appear (see Figure 4.17). Again, we follow the normal procedure of placing the independent variable in columns and the dependent variable in rows, percentages must then be based on the column totals:

- In the "Crosstabs" window (Figure 4.17), check **Column**.
- Click only **Continue**.

To find the strength of the relationship between gender and study, we need to calculate the measures of association. In the "Crosstabs" window, we have the option "Statistics," with the dialog window "Crosstabs: Statistics" (see Figure 5.1). In this window, a number of statistical functions can be chosen. When at least one of the variables is nominal, we use "Chi-square," "Phi," and "Cramér's V" as the standard choice.

- In the "Crosstabs window," click on **Statistics**.

Figure 5.1 Dialog Window "Crosstabs: Statistics"

In this dialog, one can choose from a variety of measurements of associations. The popular measurements are Cramér's *V* (when at least one variable is nominal), Kendall's Tau *b/c* (when both variables are ordinal), and Risk (e.g., to calculate the odds ratio in a 2 × 2 table).

- Check   **Chi-square**, **Phi**, and **Cramer's V**.
- Click on   **Continue**.
- Click on   **OK**.

In the output, you will find the cross-table with column percentages (see Table 4.3). As we have seen in the previous chapter, only 50% of women have chosen pedagogical sciences, which is considerably much lower than men (85.7%). In conclusion, relatively more men than women choose pedagogical sciences over educational sciences. Below that table you will find the following results (Table 5.1).

Table 5.1   The Results for Chi-Square and Cramér's V

Chi-Square Tests

	Value	df	Asymp. Sig. (2-Sided)	Exact Sig. (2-Sided)	Exact Sig. (1-Sided)
Pearson chi-square	4.952[b]	1	.026		
Continuity correction[a]	3.546	1	.060		
Likelihood ratio	5.398	1	.020		
Fisher's exact test				.040	.027
Linear-by-linear association	4.829	1	.028		
N of valid cases	40				

a. Computed only for a 2 × 2 table.

b. Zero cells (.0%) have expected count less than 5. The minimum expected count is 5.25.

Symmetric Measures

		Value	Approx. Sig.
Nominal by nominal	Phi	.352	.026
	Cramér's V	.352	.026
N of valid cases		40	

The results show that chi-square ("Pearson chi-square") is 4.952. This, however, does not indicate the strength of the relationship as the height of chi-square depends on the total number of respondents, among other factors. The measures phi and Cramér's V do not have that disadvantage: They always run between 0 (no relationship) and 1 (maximum strength). Notice that both measures have the same value. This is always the case in a table in which at least one of the variables is limited to two cases; in all other cases, Cramér's V is preferred. The value .352 indicates that there is quite a strong relationship (the maximum value of Cramér's V is 1, which is almost always impossible to achieve).

In inferential statistics, there is a so-called null hypothesis (H_0), which normally states the nonexistence of the relationship in the target population from where the sample is drawn. The alternative hypothesis (H_a) claims that there is a relationship. To test which hypothesis is more likely to be true, we have to compare the *p*-value of .026 (see under "Approx. Sig" in the lower part of Table 5.1) with the test criterion alpha (α). In many cases, this test criterion is set to .05: If *p*-values are equal or lower .05, then the null hypothesis is refuted, and consequently, the alternative hypothesis is corroborated. In many textbooks, the result is called "significant," if $p \leq \alpha$. Here, too, this is the case because .026 is lower than .05. One may even have researchers who want to test the alternative directional hypothesis saying that male students have a stronger preference to study pedagogical sciences than female students. This directional hypothesis can be tested by dividing the *p*-value by two and comparing the result with the test criterion α. Note that in many cases SPSS calculates the *p*-values for a nondirectional situation ("two-tailed testing").

5.3 Binomial Test for a Proportion △

The binominal test is designed to determine whether an observed sample proportion deviates from some expected theoretical proportion stated in the null hypothesis (H_0).

Example

Say someone claims that the fail grade of an exam in statistics is lower than .45 (or 45%). This claim is the alternative hypothesis (H_a). The null hypothesis (H_0) then says that the fail grade is .45 or higher.

- Recode the variable "grade" using **recode into different variables** (see Section 3.2). The new variable is called *"sufficient"* and has two values: 0 = lower than 5.6 and 1 = 5.6 or higher. *Note 1:* Recoding is quicker if 0–5.5 and 5.6–9 are entered as a range. *Note 2:* Some computers use a comma instead of dot for decimal depending on the language setting in Windows.
- Once you have created the new variable "sufficient," click on **Analyze, Nonparametric Test** ▶ **Legacy dialogs** ▶ **Binomial**.

The dialog window "Binomial Test" will appear (see Figure 5.1). In this window, the testing variable "sufficient" is placed into the "Test Variable" box:

- Click on the variable "sufficient," and then click →
- The default setting of the test value is .5. It must be changed to .45 (or ,45 in case of alternative decimal symbol), so click on the box next to **Test Proportion** (see Figure 5.3).
- Click on **OK**.

Figure 5.2 Dialog Window "Binomial Test"

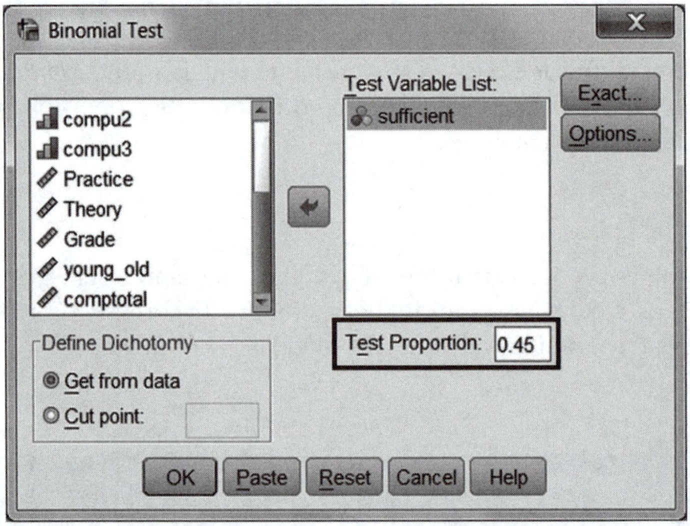

The main results of the binomial test are displayed in Table 5.2. Table 5.2 shows that the observed proportion of students who failed (Group 1, coded 0 in the variable "sufficient") the exam was .28 (11 out of 40). The likelihood, probability, or p-value was .018 (see "Asymp. Sig." in Table 5.2). So it is quite unlikely to find a proportion of .28 (or lower) in a sample while

Table 5.2 Results From a Binomial Test for a Proportion

Binomial Test

		Category	N	Observed Prop.	Test Prop.	Asymp. Sig. (1-Tailed)
Sufficient	Group 1	1.00	11	.28	.45	.018[a]
	Group 2	2.00	29	.72		
	Total		40	1.00		

a. Alternative hypothesis states that the proportion of cases in the first group < .45.

the null hypothesis is true, that is a proportion of .45 or higher in the population. If we consider the commonly used test criterion (also known as "level of significance") of .05, then the null hypothesis is refuted while the alternative hypothesis is corroborated. In other words, there is enough statistical evidence to assume that the fail grade in statistics among the population of students to be lower than .45. Note that this is one of the rare occasions when SPSS uses a one-tailed test.

5.4 One Sample *t*-Test △

A *t*-test for a sample mean is used to determine whether the value of a certain mean found in a sample deviates from an expected, theoretical mean under the null hypothesis.

Example

Suppose that nationwide studies have shown that the mean level of computer skills of students is 5.4. We hypothesize that this mean is higher among students studying pedagogical and educational sciences (the target population). To test this, follow the instructions below.

Click on   Analyze
             Compare Means ▶ One-Sample T Test.

The dialog window "One-Sample T Test" opens up, see Figure 5.3.

Figure 5.3 Dialog Window "One-Sample T Test"

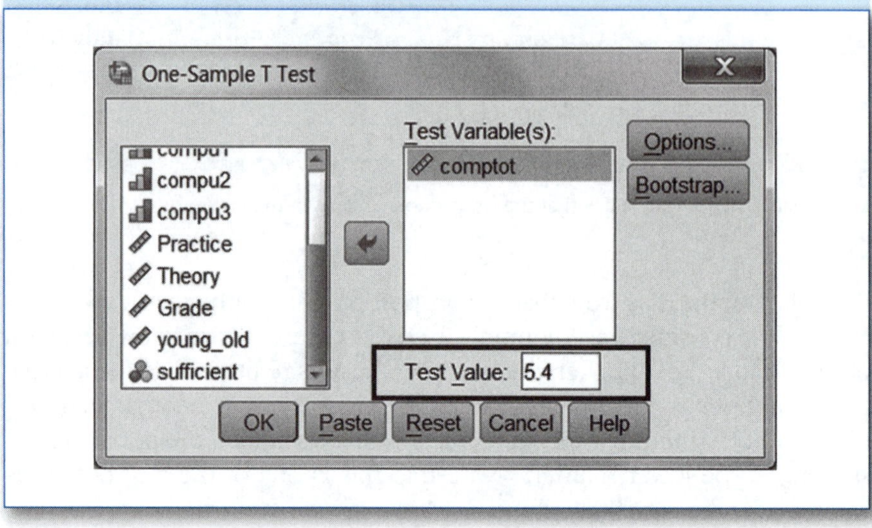

In this window, the test variable "comptot" has to be placed into the "**Test Variable(s)**" box. The default setting of the **test value** is 0. This has to be changed to 5.4.

- Place the variable "comptot" in the box with a click on the name, and then a click on ➡.
- Click on the box next to **Test Value** and change 0 to 5.4.
- Click on **OK** to execute the test.

The results are shown in Table 5.3.

The table shows the calculated mean level of computer skills, which is 8.3250. This is 2.9250 higher (see the fifth column in bottom table) compared with the test value of 5.4. The *p*-value for this difference is extremely low (lower than .001; see the fourth column in the bottom table). So it is highly unlikely to find a difference of 2.9250 in the sample whereas the mean difference in the population is actually 0 as stated in the null hypothesis. This refutes the null hypothesis: In all probability, the mean level of computer skills is larger than 5.4 in the population of pedagogical and educational science students. Note that SPSS again uses a two-tailed test. So strictly speaking, the significance value still has to be divided by 2 because the alternative hypothesis was directional (one-tailed), because we assumed the value to be *higher* than 5.4. Naturally, the test result remains the same here. In sum, the test concludes that pedagogical and educational science students have a significantly higher level of computer skills than the nationwide average of 5.4 among students.

Table 5.3 Results From a "One-Sample T Test" on Mean

One Sample Statistics

	N	Mean	Std. Deviation	Std. Error Mean
Comptot Computer skills (compu1 + 2 + 3)	40	8.3250	1.9531	.3088

One Sample Test

	Test Value = 5.4					
					95% Confidence Interval of the Difference	
	t	df	Sig. (2-Tailed)	Mean Difference	Lower	Upper
Comptot computer skills (compu1 + 2 + 3)	9.472	39	.000	2.9250	2.3004	3.5496

Finally, consider the last two columns in the bottom table in Table 5.3. The two figures give the lower and upper bound of the 95% confidence interval of the mean difference. So we also have a pretty good idea where the unknown population mean difference is to be found (there is a high probability that it is situated between 2.3004 and 3.5496).

△ 5.5 *t*-Test for Comparing Two Groups

This *t*-test is commonly used to determine whether the means within two groups deviate from each other. There are two *t*-test procedures for comparing the means of two groups. They are

1. *independent samples* t-*test*, for comparing two independent groups, and
2. *dependent samples* t-*test*, for comparing two dependent groups.

5.5.1 Independent Groups

A *t*-test for two independent groups is used to determine whether the means (of a quantitative variable) in two groups deviate from each other. Groups are statistically independent if the—randomly chosen—respondents in one group do not determine the respondents in the other. An example of independent groups would be part-time and full-time students.

Example

Suppose you want to test whether the means between part-time and full-time students differ regarding the number of practice sessions attended.

Click on   Analyze
                Compare Means ▶
                Independent-Samples T Test . . .

The "Independent-Samples T Test" window is open now; see Figure 5.4.

- Click on "practice" and place it after **Test Variable(s)** using ↴.
- In the same way, place the variable that defines the groups ("enroll") in the **Grouping Variable** box.
- Click on **Define Groups**.

The dialog window "Define Groups" will appear (see Figure 5.5).

Figure 5.4 Dialog Window "Independent-Samples T Test"

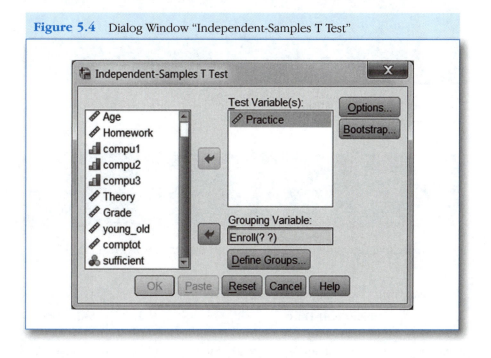

Figure 5.5 Dialog Window "Independent-Samples T Test: Define Groups"

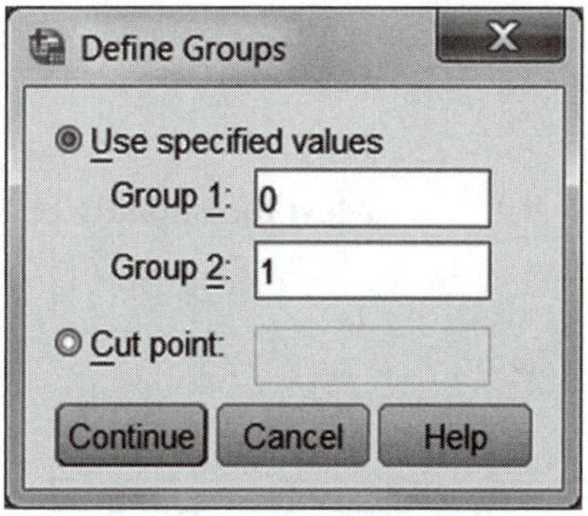

Both groups can be defined in this window:

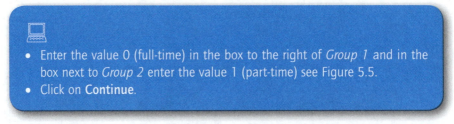

- Enter the value 0 (full-time) in the box to the right of *Group 1* and in the box next to *Group 2* enter the value 1 (part-time) see Figure 5.5.
- Click on **Continue**.

Note that the question marks in "Grouping Variable" now have been replaced by the group values 0 and 1.

Click on   **OK**.

The following results can be found in the output window (Table 5.4).

Table 5.4   Results From "Independent-Samples T Test"

	Enroll Full-Time or Part-Time	N	Mean	Std. Deviation	Std. Error Mean
Practice number of	0 Full-time	18	3.61	1.037	.244
SPSS practice lessons attained	1 Part-time	22	4.14	.941	.201

Independent Samples Test

	Levene's Test for Equality of Variances		*t*-test for Equality of Means					95% Confidence Interval of the Difference	
	F	Sig.	t	df	Sig (2-Tailed)	Mean Diff.	Std. Error Diff.	Lower	Upper
Equal variances assumed	.000	.995	−1.67	38	.102	−.5253	.313	−1.159	.10849
Equal variances not assumed			−1.66	34.82	.106	−.5253	.316	−1.167	.11675

The top table contains a number of descriptive statistic measures for both groups: number of observations, means, standard deviations, and standard errors. The bottom table displays the results of the *t*-test. There are two statistical scenarios in the table: (1) one in which the same variance is assumed for both groups ("Equal variances assumed") and (2) one in which the variances are not equal ("Equal variances not assumed"). The *F* test ("Levene's Test") is used to determine which scenario best fits the sample results. In this example, the *F*-test indicates equal variances because the *p*-value is .995 (see the third column in the bottom table), which is much higher than the usual $\alpha = .05$. This means that we do not refute the null hypothesis, which states that both groups in the target population have equal variances.

If we select equal variances, then the blue-shaded row "Equal variances assumed" in the table applies. This row shows that both means do not deviate from each other significantly in a two-tailed test and a test criterion $\alpha = .05$ because the *p*-value is .102.

5.5.2 Dependent (Paired) Groups

There is also a *t*-test for the mean difference between two dependent, or paired, groups. They are called paired groups because the—randomly chosen—respondents in one group determine the respondents in the other. Take, for example, one group consisting of children and another consisting of their mothers, a group of people who were questioned at two different points in time, or the comparison of the mean of two variables within a single group. Naturally, such tests regarding the difference in the mean are only possible if the two variables can be compared in a meaningful way. The following example compares the mean of two comparable variables within a single group, namely, the mean difference between attendance rates of theoretical lectures and practice sessions.

Example

We want to know whether students on average attended lectures more often than practice sessions.

Click on   **Analyze**
             Compare Means ▶ Paired-Samples T Test.

The dialog window "Paired-Samples T Test" will be shown (see Figure 5.6).

- Click on the variable "practice" and then click on ⬇. Repeat this instruction for the variable "theory." Now both variables appear in **"Paired Variables"** (see Figure 5.6).

Figure 5.6 Dialog Window "Paired-Samples T Test"

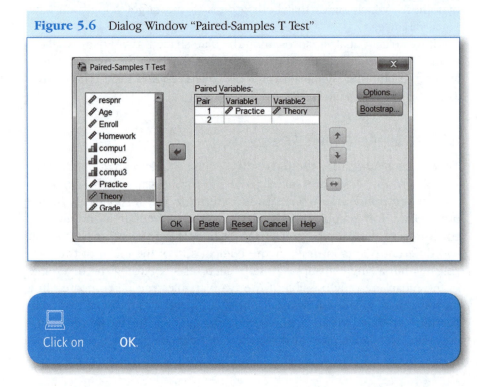

Click on   OK.

The following two tables are to be found in the output window (Table 5.5).

The mean number of practice sessions is 3.9, and the mean number of theory sessions (lectures) is 4.275, which are of concern in this case (see the top table on page 87). In a *t*-test for dependent groups, a new variable is created in SPSS, containing the differences ("Paired Difference") between the score on the variables "practice" and "theory" for each student. The

Table 5.5 Results From "Paired-Samples T Test"

Paired Sample Statistics

		Mean	N	Std. Deviation	Std. Error Mean
Pair 1	Practice in numbers	3.90000	40	1.0077	.1593
	Theory in numbers	4.2750	40	.9334	.1476

Paired Samples Test

	Paired differences							
			Std. Error Mean	95% Confidence Interval of the Difference				Sig. (2-Tailed)
	Mean	Std. Deviation		Lower	Upper	t	df	
Pair 1 Practice Theory	−.375	.49029	.07752	−.5318	−.2182	−4.837	39	.000

second (blue-shaded) column of the bottom table contains the mean of this new variable, which is −.375 (i.e., 3.9 − 4.275). So, on average, students in the sample attended fewer practice sessions than lectures.

Because we only have a sample, the difference found (−.375) may be just coincidence while the mean difference in the population is actually 0. According to the p-value ($<.001$), however, there is enough statistical evidence to support the alternative hypothesis and refute the null hypothesis (i.e., mean difference = 0). Consequently, based on a random sample of 40 students, it is most likely that the population of students in pedagogical and educational sciences on average attend more lectures than practice sessions.

We like to note that the alternative hypothesis is directional: Students on average attend *more* lectures than practice sessions. The test in SPSS is nondirectional (two-tailed), so in fact we must divide the p-value by 2, which is not necessary in this case as the p-value is already very small.

△ 5.6 Analysis of Variance

Analysis of variance (or ANOVA) is used to test whether the means in more than two independent groups deviate from each other.

Example

Assume you want to test whether the time spent on homework is equal for three distinct age groups: (1) 18 to 20 years, (2) 21 to 30 years, and (3) 31 to 37 years. To answer this research question, we use variance analysis:

- Create a new variable "age3" with **Recode into different variables** (see Section 3.2). "Age3" has three values: 1 = 18 to 20 years, 2 = 21 to 30 years, and 3 = 31 to 37 years.
- Click on   **Analyze**
               Compare Means ▶ One Way ANOVA.

The dialog window "One-Way ANOVA" opens (Figure 5.7).

Figure 5.7   Dialog Window "One-Way ANOVA"

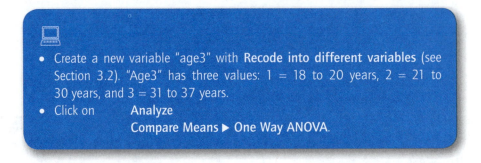

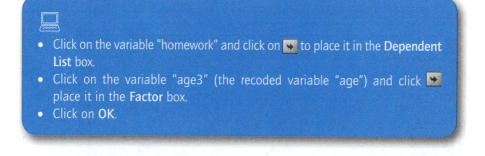

After following the instructions, the ANOVA table is displayed in the output window (Table 5.6).

Table 5.6 Results From "One-Way ANOVA"

Homework time spent on homework Statistics in hours

	Sum of Squares	df	Mean Square	F	Sig.
Between groups	456.405	2	228.203	9.026	.001
Within groups	834.345	33	25.283		
Total	1290.750	35			

The *F*-value is 9.026. The *p*-value of .001 is below the test criterion of .05, so the average amount of time they spent on homework is, in all probability, not equal across all three age groups. From the test, however, it is not clear how much the three groups differ from each other or which differences are significant. SPSS, however, does provide so-called post hoc tests, which compares and tests all mean differences. The test can be run as follows:

The dialog window "One-Way ANOVA: Post Hoc Multiple Comparisons" opens up (see Figure 5.8).

Figure 5.8   Dialog Window: "One-Way ANOVA Post Hoc Multiple Comparisons"

To test all mean differences simultaneously, the Bonferroni test is used (although there are many alternatives, see Figure 5.8).

- Click on **Bonferroni** and then click on **Continue** (see Table 5.7).
- Click on **OK**.

As a result, we get Table 5.7.

The table shows that the mean time spent on homework in the age group 18 to 20 years (Group 1) is 2.4242 minutes higher than the mean of the students in the age group 21 to 30 years (Group 2). The mean of the age group 18 to 20 years is 8.3986 minutes higher than that of the students of age group 31 years and above (Group 3). Finally, the mean of students in the age group 21 to 30 years is 5.9744 minutes higher than the mean of students in the age group 31 years and above. SPSS uses an asterisk (*) to indicate which difference is significant with $\alpha = .05$, two-tailed. In this case, these are the differences between Groups 1 and 3 (8.3986 minutes) and between Groups 2 and 3 (5.9744 minutes). Of course, we can also carry out this test

Table 5.7 Results From "Post-Hoc Multiple Comparisons: Bonferroni"

Multiple Comparisons

Dependent Variable: HOMEWORK

Bonferroni

(I) age3	(J) age3	Mean Difference (I−J)	Std. Error	Sig.	95% Confidence Interval Lower Bound	95% Confidence Interval Upper Bound
1.00	2.00	2.4242	2.0989	.769	−2.8696	7.7181
	3.00	8.3986[a]	2.0599	.001	3.2030	13.5942
2.00	1.00	−2.4242	2.0989	.769	−7.7181	2.8696
	3.00	5.9744[a]	2.0129	.017	.8974	11.0513
3.00	1.00	−8.3986[a]	2.0599	.001	−13.5942	−3.2030
	2.00	−5.9744[a]	2.0129	.017	−11.0513	−.8974

a. The mean difference is significant at the .05 level.

2-Tailed α = .05!

by comparing the *p*-values (.001 and .017) with the test criterion α = .05. In short, we can say that the students aged between 18 and 20 years and the students aged between 21 and 30 years spent significantly more time on statistics homework than the oldest group of students (31–37 years). We could not, however, find enough statistical evidence that the youngest group of students (18–20 years) spends more time on homework than the middle group of students (21–30 years) did.

Note that the asterisk (*) in Table 5.7 means "significant at α = .05 two-tailed." More often, however, you will have expectations/hypotheses on which group will score higher than the other, so you need a one-tailed test at the .05 (5%) level. This can be done easily by setting the significance level in Figure 5.1 to .10 (10%) or by dividing the significance numbers (under "Sig.") in Table 5.7 by 2.

5.7 Correlation △

The Pearson correlation is designed to determine the strength of the linear relationship between two quantitative variables (i.e., interval or ratio scaled). By linear, we mean that the relationship can be visualized as a (more or less) straight line with a gradient that is either positive or negative (see Figure 4.15 for an almost linear relationship).

Example

The number of lectures attended by a student may be related to the number of practice sessions he attends. It seems safe to hypothesize a positive relation: The more the lectures attended by a student, the higher the attendance rate of the practice sessions.

- Click on   **Analyze**
                 Correlate ▶ Bivariate . . . (see Figure 5.9).
- Double-click on "practice" (or single click on ➡).
- Double-click on "theory" (or single click on ➡).

In the dialog window "Bivarate Correlations" (Figure 5.9), both variables "theory" and "practice" are included.

Figure 5.9   Dialog Window "Bivariate Correlations"

Click on   OK.

The correlation is calculated, and the results can be found in the output window (Table 5.8).

Table 5.8   Results From "Bivariate Correlations"

Correlations		Theory	Practice
Theory number of statistical theory lessons attained	Pearson correlation	1.00	.875[a]
	Sig. (2-tailed)		.000
	N	40	40
Practice number of SPSS practice lessons attained	Pearson correlation	.875[a]	1.00
	Sig. (2-tailed)	.000	
	N	40	40

a. Correlation is significant at the 0.01 level (2-tailed).

The results show that there is a significant (p-value < .01), strong (.875; maximum is 1), and positive correlation between the number of lectures and practice sessions. The correlation is positive, so students who attend many lectures tend to follow many practice sessions and vice versa, as stated in the directional hypothesis.

5.8 Regression Analysis ▶ △

Regression analysis is used to predict and/or explain a variable with the use of one or more variables. It is assumed in this section that a linear relationship exists between the dependent (to be predicted) variable (y) and one (or more) independent variable(s) (x). This means that as in the Pearson correlation, the relationship can be visualized as a more or less straight line with a gradient that is either positive or negative (see Figure 4.15).

The following example illustrates a *simple* regression analysis in which there is one independent and one dependent variable. The analysis becomes *multiple* when other x variables are added to measure their relative impact.

5.8.1 Simple Regression Analysis

Example

Suppose we intend to find whether there is a linear relation between the total amount of time spent per week on homework and the final grade for the statistics course. We may safely hypothesize that as more time is spent on homework, the final grade for statistics will be higher.

To investigate this, follow the instructions below.

Click on   Analyze
             Regression ▶ Linear.

The dialog window "Linear Regression" will appear after this operation (Figure 5.10).

Figure 5.10   Dialog Window "Linear Regression"

In this window (see Figure 5.10), an independent variable must be specified first.

- Click on "homework" and use ⊡ to place it into in the independent variable box.
- Click on "grade" and use ⊡ to place it in the dependent variable box.
- Click on **OK**.

The results can be found in the output window and are shown below with the important information highlighted (Table 5.9).

Table 5.9 Results From "Linear Regression"

Model Summary[b]

Model	R	R Square	Adjusted R Square	Std. Error of the Estimate
1	.826[a]	.682	.673	1.0248

a. Dependent variable: Final grade received for course in statistics (1–10).

b. Predictors: (constant), homework time spent on homework statistics in hours.

Coefficients

	Unstandardized Coefficients		Standardized Coefficients		
	B	Std. Error	Beta	t	Sig.
(Constant)	−.973	.936		−1.04	.306
Homework time spent on homework statistics in hours	.244	.029	.826	8.541	.000

The top table shows the variance explained ("R Square"), which is quite high: .682 (or 68.2%), while its maximum is 1 (or 100%). Commonly, the adjusted variance ("Adjusted R Square") is used, which corrects the number of predictors (x variables) and amounts to .673 (or 67.3%). The bottom table contains the coefficients of the constant (or intercept) and the effect (gradient) of "homework." The intercept is −.973 and is the statistical grade for someone who does spend 0 minutes on homework. The constant is statistically correct but bears no relevant meaning here because such a case does not occur in our data set. The estimate (or b-coefficient) of the independent variable "homework" is .244. This means that the final grade for statistics increases with .244 points every time a student spends 1 hour (a month) more on homework. For example, if a student spends 30 hours (a month) on statistics, his or her estimated final grade is −.973 + .244 * 30 = 6.347. Given the small p-value, we can quite safely rule out the possibility that in the target population this effect of homework is actually nonexistent (0) as stated in the null hypothesis.

5.8.2 Multivariate Regression Analysis

The reason for regression analysis being one of the most popular analytical tools in social sciences is the ability to take into account more than just one predictor variable. In multivariate regression analysis, one is able to "control," or "take into account," the influence of many confounding variables and to analyze which variable has the strongest influence.

Example

Next to the positive effect of homework on the final grade for the statistics course (see the previous example), there may be other variables involved. We hypothesize that older the students are, the higher their grades. We also hypothesize female students will outperform male students, and finally we think that the more theory lessons have been attained, the higher the grade.

Click on   **Analyze**
                   Regression ▶ Linear.

In the dialog window "Linear Regression," we can add the variables of interest (note that "homework" is already in the model).

- Click on "age" and use 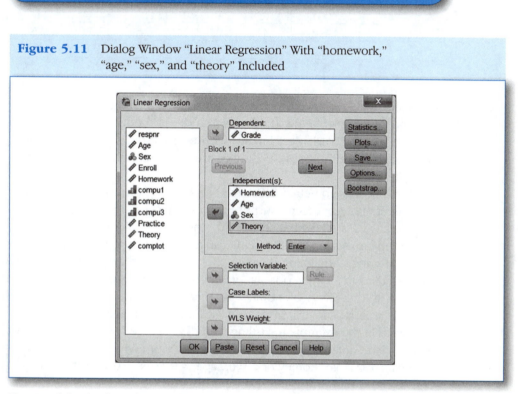 to place it in the independent variable box.
- Click on "sex" and use ⬇ to place it in the dependent variable box.
- Click on "theory" and use ⬇ to place it in the dependent variable box.
- Compare the result with Figure 5.11 and click on **OK**.

Figure 5.11 Dialog Window "Linear Regression" With "homework," "age," "sex," and "theory" Included

Note: "grade" is the dependent variable.

The results can be found in the output window, and we show the most important table here (Table 5.10).

The unstandardized coefficient of "homework" is .251: With every extra hour of homework, the grade on average is .251 points higher taking into account the confounding effects of the other variables. Student's age is negatively related to grade: The grade drops on average .003 points if a student is 1 year older, controlling for the other variables. The

Table 5.10 Results From Multivariate Linear Regression

Model	Unstandardized Coefficients		Standardized Coefficients		
	B	Std. Error	Beta	t	Sig.
(Constant)	−1.294	1.879		−.688	.496
Homework	.251	.039	.851	6.432	.000
Age	−.003	.038	−.012	−.077	.939
Sex	.490	.444	.131	1.103	.279
Theory	−.037	.249	−.016	−.150	.882

coefficient for "sex" indicates that male students (code 0) have an average score lying .490 below the female students (code 1), again controlling for the other variables. Finally, with every additional theory lesson, the average grade point is .037 lower after controlling for "homework," "age," and "sex."

The standardized beta coefficient allows for comparison in the strength of effects: It may come as no surprise that "homework" has by far the strongest effect, with "sex" coming in second, "theory" in third while "age" seems to have the lowest impact. The significance ("sig") or *p*-value is rather high in many instances, meaning that the effect found in the sample cannot be generalized to the larger population (with the test criterion of .05). The exception is the effect of homework that satisfies the condition as the *p*-value is well below .05. In sum, we cannot find corroboration for our hypotheses in the example regarding the effect of "age," "sex," and "theory" (lessons). Note that the intercept is the average score on the test with all variables being 0, that is, "homework" = 0, "age" = 0, "sex" = 0, and "theory" = 0, which is of no theoretical interest here because we do not have such students in our sample.

△ 5.9 References

Field, A. (2013). *Discovering statistics using IBM SPSS statistics (4th ed.)*. Thousand Oaks, CA: Sage.

Grotenhuis, M., & Visscher, C. (2014). *How to use SPSS syntax*. Thousand Oaks, CA: Sage.

5.10 Assignments △

1. Calculate the proportion of students who enrolled full-time in the file *chapter5fictitious.sav* (use the variable "enroll"), and test whether this proportion deviates significantly from .3 (use α = .05). Copy the results to a text file and give a brief description of your findings.
2. Calculate the average final grade (mean) for the statistics course in *chapter5fictitious.sav* (use the variable "grade"), and test whether it deviates from 6.5 in a significant way (use α = .05 again). Also copy these results to your text file and give a brief description.
3. Some claim that students who study part-time obtain lower final grades than do full-time students (use the variables "enroll" and "grade"). Test whether this claim is supported by the data using the appropriate statistical test. Again copy findings to your text file.
4. Does a (Pearson) correlation exist between "age" and the "number of practice sessions attended" ("practice")? Describe this correlation in plain words.
5. Take the variable "age3," and find out whether the three age groups differ with regard to overall computer skills ("comptot"). Also determine which age groups deviate significantly from each other. Copy the tables into the text file and describe your findings.
6. Perform a regression analysis with the overall computer skills ("comptot") as the dependent variable and the time spent on homework ("homework") as the independent variable. Place the relevant tables in your text file, and describe the linear regression results. In other words, what do the intercept and the *b*-coefficient for "homework" mean?
7. Someone tells you that the relationship between computer skills and homework is spurious and is "caused" by age (the older the student, the more computer skills and the less time spent on homework). Take the regression analysis from Question 6 and add "age" to the model (leave "homework" in the regression model). Describe briefly what has changed, and react to the claim of spuriousness.
8. Save all SPSS results as an output file, and name the file *outputchapter5*. Save the results of the tests and your descriptions in the text file and name it *text2*. Place both files in the folder **SPSS Basics**. Check whether the files *outputchapter5* and *text2* have indeed been saved. You may shut down SPSS.

For more assignments in the field of inferential statistics, please visit our website: study.sagepub.com/basicspss.

Epilogue

We conclude this handbook on SPSS with multivariate regression analysis. Of course, this does not mean that we have covered all possibilities SPSS has to offer. Instead, we addressed some commonly used applications of SPSS in the field of descriptive statistics (Chapters 2–4) and inferential statistics (Chapter 5). The SPSS programming language, which lies behind all the drop-down menus, is not covered in this book. For interested readers, we recommend our textbook *How to Use SPSS Syntax,* published by SAGE.

Naturally, the skills learned from this book are not bound to any specific field of application or research. Whether it is research on the life of Aboriginals in Australia or analytical models that deal with the relationship between eating habits and obesity: The ability to use both descriptive and inferential statistics plays a key supporting role. This gives statistical programs like SPSS a unique role in empirical quantitative research.

About IBM SPSS

T he program SPSS (originally, Statistical Package for the Social Sciences) was designed in 1968(!) and is widely used both in the field of education and academic research to enter, edit, and analyze data. Its user-friendly menus offer an extensive suite of functions that include all frequently used data modifications and statistical analyses. For more specific applications and to save all commands, the program offers the users an extensive programming language (syntax). SPSS is of IBM since 2009.

We would like to express our gratitude to IBM SPSS for making all the figures and tables in this book available to us.

For more information about SPSS and the availability of trial versions (valid for 14 days) of the program, please visit the SPSS website: http://www-01.ibm.com/software/analytics/spss/

Index

SAGE researchmethods

The essential online tool for researchers from the world's leading methods publisher

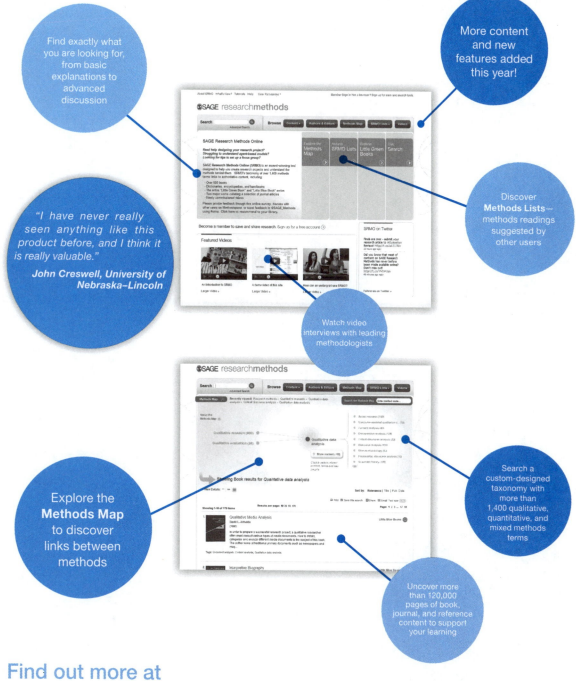

Find exactly what you are looking for, from basic explanations to advanced discussion

More content and new features added this year!

Discover **Methods Lists**—methods readings suggested by other users

"I have never really seen anything like this product before, and I think it is really valuable."

John Creswell, University of Nebraska–Lincoln

Watch video interviews with leading methodologists

Explore the **Methods Map** to discover links between methods

Search a custom-designed taxonomy with more than 1,400 qualitative, quantitative, and mixed methods terms

Uncover more than 120,000 pages of book, journal, and reference content to support your learning

Find out more at
www.sageresearchmethods.com